D0069451

Arguing Constructively

Dominic A. Infante
Kent State University

WAVELAND
PRESS, INC.
Prospect Heights, Illinois

Consulting Editors

Joseph A. DeVito
Robert E. Denton, Jr.

For information about this book, write or call:
Waveland Press, Inc.
P.O. Box 400
Prospect Heights, Illinois 60070
(312) 634-0081

Copyright © 1988 by Waveland Press, Inc.

ISBN 0-88133-327-1

All rights reserved. No part of this book may be reproduced, stored in a retrieval system, or transmitted in any form or by any means without permission in writing from the publisher.

Printed in the United States of America

7   6   5   4   3   2

To Sandy

Contents

PART III
ARGUMENTATIVE REFINEMENTS

Preface

This book has a dual focus. On the one hand, the purpose is to instruct on the methods of argumentation theory. This represents a set of principles, methods, and strategies of argument which have evolved from the time of Ancient Greece. On the other hand, the intent is to teach human relations in argumentative situations, specifically, how to manage interpersonal relations during arguments. These ideas are more contemporary, resulting mainly from fairly recent research.

Because of the dual focus, this book is a bit unusual. Books on argumentation and debate have tended to say little about how arguing can affect the relationship you have with your adversary. How do you prevent harm to a valued friendship, for instance? Moreover, books on interpersonal communication have little to say about arguing. Instead, the emphasis is on achieving satisfying relations with others. This, of course, ignores the fact that two people advocating conflicting positions on an issue while attempting to refute one another's position is a common form of interpersonal communication. You recognize this form as *argument*; many of the significant situations in our lives are typified by people holding and emphasizing different views. Thus, argument is both a frequent and an integral component in the study of interpersonal communication.

Why the book is unusual, then, is that it is a *hybrid* text, a

term given to communication books which attempt to deal with
and to integrate two or more areas of communication studies.
This was done because I believe it is time to bring the two
areas together. Teaching only argumentation and debate
theory has limitations because application focuses on formal
legislative and judicial settings. However, arguing
constructively in informal interpersonal and small group
contexts is a skill that can result in numerous good outcomes.
Moreover, interpersonal communication instruction on
building and maintaining satisfying relations with other people
is lacking if it does not deal with how to do this while arguing,
especially since argumentative communication probably will
occur throughout a relationship. Thus, this book was written to
correct what I think has been too narrow a focus in the areas of
argumentation and interpersonal communication. Or, to put it
another way, there is more to these two areas of communication than has been realized. Recent research, which will
be discussed, makes it clear that argumentation and interpersonal communication are complementary areas of
communication.

This text may be used in argumentation courses that do not
have a formal debate emphasis. However, it could be used as a
supplement in "traditional" debate courses in order to
introduce the student to a more comprehensive experience
with argumentation. The book should be especially appropriate
for the basic course in communication and also for
interpersonal communication. Since I contend that *arguing is a
basic skill*, it should be taught early in the communication
curriculum because it is foundational for many other forms of
communication such as public speaking, group discussion,
interviewing, bargaining, and negotiation.

This material may be used in a variety of other courses in
disciplines of the social sciences which are concerned with
improving the individual's social effectiveness. For instance,
courses in psychology or education which offer assertiveness
training may want to consider an argumentative approach.
Generally, I think you will find the principles of argumentation
theory more specific, systematic, and less situationally-bound
than the techniques of assertiveness training.

The subject matter may also be used for self-study by

individuals who are motivated to improve how they communicate in conflict situations. You do not have to be enrolled in a college class to learn the art of arguing constructively. You can study the book on your own, work through the exercises at the end of each chapter, and then employ the principles in your daily interactions. These interactions provide a laboratory for experimenting with changes in your communication behavior. The principles and examples are clear enough, I believe, so that you can move toward improvements with confidence. If you are studying this book on your own, you might want to see if a spouse, close friend, or a colleague would like to work through the book with you. This would not only benefit them but would also facilitate your acquisition of new skills by the stimulus of a "training partner." This is a concept borrowed from physical fitness: two people stimulate one another to work longer and harder; you tend not to miss a workout because you feel a sense of obligation to the other person.

I would like to acknowledge several people who influenced my thinking greatly on the subject of this book. Three individuals taught me the basic principles of constructive argumentation and all I had to do after their tutelage was to acquire some refinements. The first was my high school debate coach, the late Mr. E.J. Diller of Youngstown Chaney High School in Ohio. The others were my college debate coaches at Bowling Green State University, Dr. Raymond Yeager and Dr. Otto Bauer. In addition, I would like to thank several people who, through their collaboration and friendship, have shaped my research program on arguing and verbal aggression. Two are former doctoral students. Dr. Andrew S. Rancer of Emerson College in Boston developed a theory of argumentativeness with me and has been my co-author on several articles. Dr. Charles J. Wigley III of Canisius College in Buffalo worked with me in developing our recent model of verbal aggressiveness. I would also like to thank my colleague, Dr. William I. Gorden, of Kent State University. We have collaborated on research for the past ten years, and he has given to me and stimulated in me more ideas than I can count.

Finally, I would like to thank my family. My daughter, Laura, and my son, Jeffrey, gave me love, pride, and also humility. On numerous occasions as they were growing up, I used the principles in this book in a way that I thought approached perfection only to have my arguments, about some aspect of their behavior or desired behavior, totally deflected by the cognitive armor which teenagers wear. This helped keep me humble. My wife, Sandy, has been extremely important to me in more ways that I can ever acknowledge. In terms of this book, over the years she has helped keep me "argumentatively fit." She was not on the debate team in high school or college, so I taught her how to argue. As it turned out, however, I may have taught her too well for it is seldom that I win an argument with her!

PART I

UNDERSTANDING ARGUING

1

Argumentativeness
Your Constructive Side

In your years of interacting with people, you probably have been involved in arguments over controversial issues which were very stimulating, challenging, and constructive. Because interest and enjoyment is so high in such situations, it could be concluded that there are few more rewarding ways of interacting with people.

Contrasted with these pleasant experiences, however, are encounters which we would like to forget. All of us probably have participated in arguments which resulted in hurt feelings, anger, frustration, confusion, embarrassment, and even damaged or broken interpersonal relationships. Perhaps you have been involved in an argument which ended with physical violence. Such experiences may have led you to conclude that arguing is a destructive form of communication which should be avoided. You might even be one of many people who repress their true feelings and their best interests in order to keep an argument from happening. Some people seem to go almost to any length to dodge a potential argument.

This book will deal with the baffling matter that arguments can be one of our very best communication experiences or one of the very worst. We will explain this seeming puzzle by examining the aggressive side of our personality. Generally, what we will see is that the aggressive dimension of our personality has several facets. Some are constructive, but others are destructive. Once we understand our constructive aggressive traits, we can specify procedures for learning those behaviors and thus increase how constructive we are in conflict situations. Also, understanding our destructive tendencies will permit us to identify the behaviors which are at fault and provide ways to reduce destructive behavior in conflict situations.

I am contending that all arguments should be constructive, stimulating, positive experiences and that the destructive, negative experiences can be avoided. This book is designed around that contention. The purpose is to teach you how to argue constructively and how to control what happens so arguments do not become destructive. As you will see a little later in this chapter, knowing how to argue is a valuable social skill which can result in many benefits for you. Thus, another contention is that you should argue and that excessive avoidance of arguments can have a harmful effect on the quality of your life.

A reason why this skill is important is that it is an effective tool for dealing with the controversies in your life. Controversy exists when you and at least one other person realize your positions on an issue are incompatible. This probably occurs more than once each day of your life. With a husband and wife, for example, controversy may begin in the morning (e.g., Who should cook breakfast?), extend into the afternoon (e.g., Should a spouse play golf instead of doing household chores?), spill over into the evening (e.g., What television programs should we watch?), and culminate at bedtime (e.g., Whose fault was it that so little was accomplished today?).

There is not only one way of dealing with controversy. There are several appropriate approaches. An *informative approach* entails the individuals stating their positions on an issue in order to let one another know where they stand. That is, your only real concern is that you want the other person to have information about your position on the issue and to use that information as he or she sees fit. A *persuasive approach* to controversy involves at least one person explaining his or her position on an issue and the reasons for that position in order to influence the other person to agree. An *argumentative approach* involves informative and persuasive aspects. In addition, each person attacks the other's position on the issue in order to establish the superiority of one's own position.

What do you do, typically, when you recognize the potential for controversy in a situation? Do you nearly always engage in argumentative communication? If you do, you probably argue too much. This book claims arguing is good for you. However, arguing, like most things in life, requires restraint and moderation in order to realize maximum benefits. A person who is too willing to clash verbally with other people is usually perceived as quarrelsome, too aggressive, too combative, unaccommodating and unfriendly.

At the other extreme, do you almost never speak up when you realize your position on an issue conflicts with that of another person? If so, you probably are too compliant, too timid, and as a result you allow things to happen which sometimes are not in your best interests. Arguing enables you to exert some control over your life. Avoiding arguments tends to encourage other people to have their way, and you are left with the unsettling feeling that they have taken advantage of your easygoing, agreeable manner.

A more desirable style is between these two extremes. As we said, controversy is seldom absent from our daily routines. Often, we can deal with the issue by informing the other person of our position. At other times, we can attempt persuasion but not push the interaction as far as an argument.

A number of factors could motivate us to argue. We might believe the issue is vital to our self-interest. We may see the controversy as what is in the best interests of the other person or a third party not involved in the argument. Intense curiosity may stimulate an argument, e.g., what really happened? We might argue because we desire to solve a problem, e.g., how can tax reform be accomplished best? We argue to improve cooperation, a vital process in society that has enabled much progress, e.g., who should do what? Entertainment is also a valid reason to argue. Arguing political issues or religion (even though an adage says never argue these things) can be more fun than many of the games people play together for amusement. As with all contests or games, however, all parties should want to play. A game is less than satisfying if you are forced to play.

Before we begin focusing on arguing in this book, it is necessary to emphasize that you should not always argue when controversy arises in social situations. You should strive for *variety* and *balance* in your communication style for dealing with controversy. At times you should be able to handle controversy by simply being informative. At other times persuasion is the most appropriate choice. Sometimes it is necessary to argue. On still other occasions, the most prudent way of managing controversy is to say nothing. Silence can be a most appropriate communication tactic. This book is about arguing and develops the idea that arguing is good for you, but only under certain conditions and when arguments are conducted in a certain manner.

Aggressive Communication

In order to understand the mixture of good and bad experiences we have had while arguing, it is necessary to examine the aggressive dimension of our personalities. In a recent chapter (Infante, 1987), I developed a model of aggressiveness in interpersonal communication. Aggressiveness occurs in physical or symbolic forms which are either constructive or destructive. Constructive elements produce satisfaction and improve the interpersonal relationship while destructive forms produce dissatisfaction and deteriorate the relationship.

Examples of constructive physical aggression are sports or playfulness as in mock assaults. Destructive types of physical aggression include violence against persons (e.g., battery, murder, rape) and violence against objects (e.g., throwing an object in rage).

Symbolic aggression is the major focus of the model and means using verbal and nonverbal channels in order, minimally, to dominate and perhaps damage, or maximally, to defeat and perhaps destroy another person's positions on topics of communication and/or the person's self-concept. These behaviors, attacks on a person's position or a person's self-concept, are viewed as a product of the aggressiveness dimension of the individual's personality. The aggressive personality is conceived as having four facets, two are constructive and two are destructive.

The constructive facets are *assertiveness* and *argumentativeness*. Assertiveness is defined as a general tendency to be interpersonally dominant, ascendant, and forceful. Behavior of this type takes many forms, e.g., a defense of your rights such as asking someone not to smoke, taking leadership responsibilities in group situations, initiating a conversation with a stranger, resisting pressure to conform to a group opinion. Argumentativeness includes the ability to recognize controversial issues in communication situations, to present and defend positions on the issues, and to attack the positions which other people take (Infante and Rancer, 1982). Assertiveness is a broad trait which includes argumentativeness, a more specific trait. Thus, all arguing is assertive behavior, but not all assertiveness involves arguing.

The destructive facets of the aggressiveness dimension of personality are *hostility* and *verbal aggressiveness*. Hostility is defined as using symbols (verbal or nonverbal) to express irritability, negativism, resentment, and suspicion. It is easy to construct situations where these four destructive tendencies would apply. An example of hostile feelings stemming from resentment would be "I am deeply offended that I did not get the promotion and I will hold this against those responsible!" Verbal aggressiveness is defined as the inclination to attack the self-concepts of individuals instead of, or in addition to, their positions on particular issues (Infante & Wigley, 1986). There are many types of verbally aggressive messages. We will examine them in the next chapter. Verbally aggressive messages commonly include: "You have to be stupid to believe that." "You are absolutely worthless." "They are in bad shape if they have to rely on you." Parallel to the discussion regarding constructive traits, hostility is more global while verbal aggressiveness is more specific. Thus, all verbal aggression is hostile, but not all hostility involves attacking the self-concepts of other people.

One explanation, then, for the mixture of experiences we have had when arguing would be that all of the behavior was not genuine argument. Actual argument involves presenting and defending a position on a controversial issue and attacking the positions which others take. Attack and defend stances are taken by the people involved *only* with respect to the individuals' positions on the issue. There are no attacks on other people in order to hurt them psychologically or to make them question their self-worth; people should not be made to feel that they must defend themselves. When that does happen, the discussion turns into the *counterfeit* of genuine argument because verbal aggression has shifted the attack and defend stances which people take in conflict situations from the person's position to the person's self-concept. This shift in the locus of attack from position to self-concept results in the discussion shifting from constructive to destructive, and our feeling about the discussion changes from favorable to unfavorable.

Knowing this we can say that *in order to have constructive arguments we should follow the principles of argumentation.* This book will explain those principles. Further, to avoid destructive verbal clashes, we need to control verbal aggression. This can be done by understanding verbal aggression better (the topic of the next chapter) and learning what to do when verbal aggression is used in a discussion (Chapter 7).

The Value of Arguing

Johnson and Johnson (1979) reviewed over 100 articles and concluded that arguing appears to have constructive outcomes for the individual. Arguing stimulates our curiosity about the topics of argument and this increases learning because we seek more information about the issues we have disputed. Egocentric thinking (seeing oneself at the center of everything) is reduced by arguing since the topics must be examined from multiple viewpoints and this discourages the individual from relating a subject only to self. Arguing improves social perspective-taking (seeing something from another person's perspective), a skill which is vital to communication effectiveness and social intelligence. Creativity is stimulated by arguing because of the heightened favorable arousal. The quality of decision-making and problem-solving in groups is enhanced by argument.

Research has also found specific communication effects of arguing. People experienced in argument are perceived as more dynamic when they argue, more expert in the topic even though they might not know more about it than anyone else, more interested in the communication situation, and more skillful arguers (Infante, 1981). Other research has found highly argumentative individuals are more difficult to provoke into the use of verbal aggression when the opponent is very stubborn (Infante, Trebing, Shepherd, & Seeds, 1984). This is an interesting result because we know it is relatively easy to say something "nasty" to a person who is being stubborn. Research with married couples has found that happily married couples argue in a constructive manner while those who are unhappily married argue in a destructive way (Gottman, 1979). Research in the work setting has discovered the more subordinates perceived their superiors to be high in argumentativeness and low in verbal aggressiveness, the more the subordinates were satisfied with their job and supervisor (Infante & Gorden, 1985a). Another study found that supervisors who were more argumentative had more favorable job outcomes (such as higher salaries) and more career satisfaction. An implication from this research is that the ability to argue skillfully may be a vital ingredient for success in many work situations and professions. Increasing the argumentativeness of women who were low in argumentativeness resulted in a significant increase in their credibility (Infante, 1985). A study by Onyekwere (1986) found more argumentative people were more competent communicators in a discussion. Schultz (1982) discovered leadership in group situations was associated with individuals who were more argumentative. Other group research by Nemeth (1986) suggests an argumentative minority improves group problem-solving and decision-making even if it is not persuasive with the majority because more careful, critical consideration of issues is stimulated. In essence, the majority is forced to exert more cognitive effort which leads to more thoroughness.

You can see from this summary of research that there are benefits to arguing. You probably will be a more effective person socially and more successful in general if you develop the aggressive part of your personality that is constructive— assertiveness and argumentativeness. The purpose of this text is to enhance your argumentativeness. You can begin a program of improving your assertiveness by examining books by Alberti and Emmons (1974) and Adler (1977).

Overview of the Book

This book is divided into three sections. The first is introductory and is designed to create a very clear distinction between arguing and verbal aggression. Knowing the difference and keeping the two separate is crucial to achieving the primary goal of the author—to teach you to argue constructively. The first two chapters will sharply distinguish argument from verbal aggression. The point is not made and then dropped. The idea will be reinforced throughout the book.

The second section of the book will teach you constructive argumentation. Learning how to argue constructively is divided into five parts. Each part specifies a group of skills related to competent argumentation. Taken together, the skills represent a conception of *argumentative competence*. Each of these parts of the process of argumentation is covered in detail in a chapter. A brief overview of the five parts is presented in order to give you a sampling of what is involved when arguing constructively.

The first part of argumentative competence involves *stating the controversy in propositional form*. This is not just an academic exercise. By formulating a proposition which specifies what is being argued, you provide clear direction for the argument. You realize who is pro and who is con on a particular proposition, who has the burden of proof, who has the benefit of presumption, and finally whether in fact you have an argument. That is, in formulating a proposition we sometimes realize we and our potential adversary hold the same position. Or we find out that while we want to argue one thing, the other person is intent on arguing something different. Thus, the first task is to agree on the issue of disagreement.

Without this skill, arguments are unproductive since the arguers do not really understand the other's position. This part also deals with preparing for arguments, especially reading habits and orientations to information-seeking which are helpful in providing useful knowledge for arguments.

The second portion of skillful argumentation is concerned with *analyzing the proposition and inventing arguments* to support your position and attack the other person's position. This is a skill which is especially critical to arguing well since, it should go without saying, success in argumentation depends upon having good arguments. While some people seem to be born with the ability to come up with impressive ideas, the rest of us have to learn how to do this. We will learn an inventional system which studies have found to be significantly effective in stimulating people to discover arguments. An inventional system is a systematic way of thinking about a topic which creates issues leading to specific arguments about the topic.

The third part of competent argumentation involves *presenting and defending your position.* We will focus on the major strategies for favoring a proposition and the strategies for opposing the proposition. These represent the overall strategies, or types of cases, which you can utilize in an argument. On a more specific level, I will explain how to present a single argument. This is a four-step procedure which has proven effective over years of use in competitive debating and is fairly easy to use. Defending your position is called rebuttal and skill in this area is essential in order to succeed in arguments. Our focus here will be on a four-step procedure for rebuilding an argument and the various strategies to use in this process. We will also emphasize evaluating your position in general, communicating clearly how your position survived your opponent's attack, and why it is the superior position on the topic.

The fourth portion of arguing consists of *attacking other positions.* This is called refutation and is an exciting part of argumentation since it involves verbal clash with another person. As with the other parts of argumentative competence, this one is very systematic and makes use of a number of well-tested procedures and strategies. We will work with a four-step procedure for attacking another person's argument. A dozen strategies for attacking your opponent's reasoning and evidence will be studied.

The fifth part of being a competent arguer involves *managing interpersonal relations* during an argument. Quite simply, the concern is how to damage your opponent's position without damaging the opponent. As explained earlier, verbal aggression has no place in the process of rational discourse. An argument should consist of only genuine argument as specified by the first four parts of our model of argumentative competence. We will examine numerous techniques and strategies for keeping arguments friendly, pleasant, and constructive. Also, we will learn several tactics for dealing with verbal aggression when it does occur.

The third section of this book contains two chapters which cover a variety of additional factors of consequence in the argumentative situation. One such issue is analyzing your adversaries so you can adapt your arguments to their values. We will also discuss presentational factors such as organization, delivery, language, and nonverbal behavior. All of these constitute *refinements* to the essentials of argumentation which you will learn in the second section of the book. The third section, then, focuses on polishing basic skills and fine-tuning them to maximize your effectiveness in argumentative situations.

Orientation to the Approach

It is very important for you to realize that although we will examine these five parts of argumentative competence one at a time, they function as facets of a whole and thus their true significance will not be apparent until you become at least minimally proficient as an arguer. Also, there is an awkwardness and confusion when you begin to learn something and must concentrate on the various parts individually. This is somewhat like when you are learning to play golf. You are taught "parts" of the game: grip, stance, swing, chipping, putting, etc. Once you are able to hit the ball solidly on nearly every shot, you do not feel as awkward or so confused. You are aware of grip, stance, etc. However, since you have mastered these parts at least somewhat, you are not distracted by them.

You will need some patience in learning how to argue effectively. Argumentation is like other highly skilled activities. It is complex. Nevertheless, it can be learned readily by individuals with average intelligence. An exciting prospect, according to our research, is that if you are "average" in intelligence, learning to argue constructively can result in other people perceiving you as "above average" in intelligence.

Like other skills, arguing can be broken into a number of parts — five, according to my approach. Each part can be learned individually. Then, we put the parts together to constitute the whole; that is, argumentation. There is some awkwardness and confusion initially. However, before long the parts become synchronized and function smoothly as an integrated unit. When this happens, you have acquired a new social skill.

It is important to realize that this skill — effective argumentation — is a very valuable *social tool*. It is a method to use in conflict situations where you want one thing and another person wants something else. The argumentative, informative, and persuasive approaches to disagreement explained are superior to common tactics which are used in social conflict situations. One of those tactics to be avoided is verbal aggression. As we shall see in the next chapter, attacking a person's self-concept produces a number of effects, all of which are destructive. You will have little success in conflict situations if you rely upon verbal aggression.

Another common tactic which people use is compliance-gaining strategies (Miller, Boster, Roloff, & Seibold, 1977). Examples are the use of threats, promises, rewards, guilt, debt, etc. These tactics will sometimes succeed in getting a person to do what you are proposing. However, people generally will have less favorable feelings toward your proposal and less respect for you when you utilize this type of strategy.

Physical force, or the threat of it, is sometimes used in conflict situations (for a review of aggression research see Bandura, 1973; Berkowitz, 1962; Buss, 1961; Zillman, 1979).

While physical force may work at times, people will have no respect for you or your ideas. Do not confuse fear with respect. Physical force can produce fear, but it rarely results in positive regard. Additionally, the use of force increases the level of stress a person experiences. The anxiety produced by the possibility that one's victim will retaliate will undoubtedly lessen the quality of one's life. Also, people who use physical force tend to feel inadequate; failing to use their intelligence to solve a problem can lead to feeling "dumb" about resorting to force.

Finally, people sometimes do nothing in conflict situations (see Folger & Poole, 1984; Jandt, 1973; Wilmot & Wilmot, 1978). Avoidance or silence sometimes is the most appropriate response to a controversial topic. However, people who habitually respond that way may be too compliant and thus sacrifice their best interests and their rights in order to avoid "clashing" with other people. So, avoidance and silence tactics can cheat individuals out of what they have coming to them. People who do not like the idea of clashing with other people will see that the methods of argumentation taught in this book are not distasteful and can be used by individuals who consider themselves to be very gentle, easygoing, and peaceful. Using genuine argument does not mean engaging in a "shouting match" with your adversary. An excellent argument may be spoken very low-keyed, with little sense of urgency. Do not conclude that to use and to benefit from argumentation theory one must be extremely dynamic, outgoing, and aggressive. One of the nice characteristics of constructive argumentation is that it really is for everyone.

Summary

Four approaches to dealing with controversy were discussed: informative, persuasive, argumentative, and avoidance. Moderation was emphasized in terms of being argumentative. Argumentativeness was examined within the context of a recent model of the aggressive personality. The model discusses a cluster of four traits, two are constructive and two are destructive. The constructive traits are argumentativeness and assertiveness while the destructive traits are verbal aggressiveness and hostility. The model was used to explain the seeming paradox of some arguments being very positive while others are very negative. The constructive facets of the aggressive dimension of personality tend to control positive argumentative experiences while the destructive facets energize negative episodes. An extensive body of research was reviewed which revealed numerous benefits of arguing. This suggested the idea that avoiding argumentative communication deprives one of possible benefits. An overview of the three parts of the book introduced a five-part model of argumentative competence which serves as the basis for the book. The approach emphasizes breaking the skill, arguing, into parts which are then integrated into a whole. Effective argumentation, as a social tool in conflict situations, was contrasted with the generally undesirable methods of verbal aggression, compliance strategies, physical force, and silence or avoidance which is sometimes undesirable.

Exercises

1. In order to understand your argumentative behavior better, complete the Argumentative Scale which is in Appendix A at the end of the book.
2. After completing the Argumentativeness Scale, turn to Appendix B for the scoring instructions and interpretation of scores. Follow the instructions and compute your argumentativeness scores. Then use the classification information to determine whether your score was high, moderate, or low.
3. Administer the Argumentativeness Scale to a close friend, husband or wife. Compare your scores. Are the two of you similar or different in terms of the tendency to argue? Was one person lower than the other by one or more categories (e.g., one person moderate, the other high)? If so, does the difference hurt or help your relationship? Discuss arguing

with this person. What should be the role of arguing in your relationship? Be specific in terms of what you want in the relationship regarding argumentative behavior.

4. If this book is being used in a class in which you are enrolled, divide the class into groups of about five persons each. Discuss one or more of the following questions:

    a. How would it benefit me to improve my argumentative behavior?

    b. What aspects of my argumentative behavior seem to need the most improvement?

    c. What reservations do I have about becoming more argumentative?

    d. In what ways am I too argumentative?

    Have someone in each group prepare a summary of the ideas discussed. Present the summary to the entire class for discussion.

5. If you are not enrolled in a class, examine the questions in #4 by yourself. Write your answers in a notebook which you can also use for the other exercises in this book.

2

Verbal Aggressiveness
Your Destructive Side

Argumentation and verbal aggression may be viewed as *opposing forces* when controversial topics are discussed. When self-concept attacks are introduced into a discussion, argumentation is inhibited. It is very difficult to practice argumentation when verbal aggression becomes part of a discussion. On the other hand, our contention is that when the methods of constructive argument are employed by all parties in an argument the practice of verbal aggression is inhibited. Hence, one discourages the other.

Recognizing these opposing forces allows us to distinguish three types of verbal clashes. Two are destructive and one is constructive. Once we learn to recognize the types, we will be in a better position to control them, and that is a major purpose of this book — to reduce the occurrence of destructive arguments in your life.

The following are examples of the three types of verbal clashes:

Husband: I'm looking forward to a vacation this summer.
Wife: Me too. Let's do something exciting.
Husband: I want to do what we always do, take our boat to Lake Erie for two weeks and go from one island to another.

Wife: That's stupid! You never want to do anything different. It's always the same boring
thing, year after year.

Husband: Well I think there's something wrong with
you! All you want is excitement. Maybe
you're really a closet jetsetter!

Wife: But, at least I'm not selfish. You decide what
you want with no consideration of my needs.

Husband: I'm selfish? What about you? You're the one
who decides where we go every week on our
night out.

This is an example of pure verbal aggression. Once different
positions on the topic of communication were recognized, the
individuals began attacking one another's character and never
let up. This is a destructive form of communication. Even if the
couple in our example later kiss, make up, and feel very close
after apologies are made, damage has been done. There are
better ways of achieving intimacy.

Consider a second type of verbal clash:

Husband: I'm looking forward to a vacation this
summer.

Wife: Me too. Let's do something exciting.

Husband: What did you have in mind?

Wife: We could fly to Las Vegas and go to shows
and the casinos.

Husband: Well, I would prefer taking our boat to Lake
Erie and touring the islands.

Wife: We've done that so many years, though, I'm
afraid we are going to get into a rut. And
they say such repetition isn't healthy for a
relationship.

Husband: I can appreciate that. But, the cost of your
idea would be at least five times what it
would cost to do our usual. We can't afford
such an expensive vacation. You just don't
have a sense of responsibility when it comes
to the money I earn.

Wife: I don't squander "your" money! Besides, its
our money. You're neurotic about money, a

real tightwad. Charles Dickens could have
used you as the model for his Scrooge
character.

In this example, argumentation and verbal aggression were
mixed. The existence of these two opposing forces in the
discussion created a destructive exchange of ideas. This may
be the most common form of destructive communication. The
interaction begins in a healthy manner but degenerates into a
verbal sluggfest, with the individuals' self-concepts absorbing
the punishment. Did you recognize when the shift from
argument to verbal aggression took place?

Now for our third example. Imagine, in the second example,
that the husband ended his third speech with the claim—"We
can't afford such an expensive vacation"—and the verbal
aggression in the last sentence was not spoken. Let us pick up
the action from there.

Wife: I've checked out the prices. The travel agen-
cy has a packaged tour, and it's really not
very expensive.

Husband: True. Airfair, hotel, and meals may be reasonable. But gambling is not included. I
don't know of anyone who has ever resisted
gambling once they are there and get caught
up in the excitement. That could very well
be the most expensive vacation of our lives.

Wife: I think you are overly emphasizing the danger. You and I simply are not compulsive
gamblers. We could easily establish a very
modest budget for gambling and when it's
gone consider that portion of our vacation
complete.

Husband: Are you that confident that we will not get
caught up in the atmosphere?

Wife: Sure.

Husband: Well, how about considering another idea?
Instead of the usual fishing, swimming, eat-
ing and sleeping on the boat, what if we go
out to eat in the good restaurants by the

marinas? And, we could dock at one of the
yacht clubs in Cleveland and go to a baseball game, a play, maybe a concert?

This discussion remained focused on the controversial
issue — where to vacation. It was a genuine argument. Only
argumentation was employed. The participants did not attack
one another's self-concept. The individuals defended different
positions on the topic and attacked the other person's position.
Reasons were given for the attacks. Some of the reasons
contained little fact and seemed to be more emotional
reactions. However, emotion directed at a controversial topic
can be an acceptable tactic in an argument. We are not saying
the quality of the arguments in the third example was
excellent. However, the discussion was constructive and
serves as one example of what this book will attempt to
teach — constructive argument.

Verbal aggression, as we said, involves attacking another
person's self-concept. This does not mean we should never
discuss another person's self-concept with him or her. It is
possible to have a genuine argument which focuses on your
self-concept and/or the other person's self-concept. The
controversial issue might be, "am I too dominant in our
relationship?" or "are you too fearful of failure?" Such
discussions are usually extremely important when they occur.
However, great care must be taken. Self-concept issues are
especially delicate and there is a particular danger that the
discussion will stimulate feelings of defensiveness, or even
degenerate into verbal aggressiveness. Since self-concept
issues do need to be discussed at times in an interpersonal
relationship, it is important to learn methods of making
discussions about these issues constructive.

Verbal Aggression

When an individual's self-concept is attacked instead of, or
in addition to, that person's position on a topic of
communication, the individual is a victim of verbal aggression
(Infante & Wigley, 1986). A verbally aggressive message is

designed to produce psychological pain, to have the person feel less favorably about self. Such a message is sometimes called a "put-down."

Whether or not a given message in interpersonal communication is seen as verbally aggressive can vary according to the individuals in a dyad, observers, and society. If a person meant a message to be verbally aggressive, but the receiver of the message does not see the message as a personal attack, the message is verbally aggressive according to the sender. On the other hand, a message might not be intended as verbally aggressive by the sender but will be perceived as a personal attack by the receiver. In that case, the message is verbally aggressive according to the receiver's perspective. This type of noncorrespondence can occur when there is an observer of the dyad. The observer might think verbal aggression was used, but the dyad members might not. Nevertheless, from the observer's perspective, verbal aggression occurred. Society's view could be noncorrespondent with the individuals in a dyad. For instance, one person might say he or she was verbally provoked into an act of physical violence against another person, but society (e.g., a court of law in this case) might disagree.

The answer, then, to the issue of how do we determine verbal aggression is not simple. Several vantage points for an exchange of messages between two people are possible: the individuals involved, observers, and society. Contending that any of these perspectives is invalid appears indefensible. Thus, all should be considered. Allowing for multiple viewpoints raises the possibility that persons will not agree. That, I believe, is preferable to an overly simplistic notion of what constitutes verbal aggression. Besides, if two people disagree on whether a message was verbally aggressive, that is a legitimate topic for constructive argument.

Verbally aggressive messages come in a variety of forms. In recent articles (Infante, 1987; Infante & Wigley, 1986), the following typology has been developed.

Character Attacks	Teasing
Competence Attacks	Ridicule
Insults	Profanity
Maledictions	Threats

Background Attacks   Nonverbal Indicators
Physical Appearance Attacks

You probably recognize the first ten types without much
difficulty. The last, "nonverbal indicators," may seem to be out
of place since we are concerned with "verbal" aggression.
However, a nonverbal indicator can be equivalent to a word
and thus constitute a verbal message. Examples of nonverbal
messages which actually take the place of verbal messages are
shaking a clenched fist, a look of disgust, shaking the head in
disbelief, a look of contempt, rolling the eyes, a deep sigh, and
tone of voice. All of these can tell a person he or she is
incompetent, of low character, or can imply a threat. An angry
tone of voice, for example, can be verbally aggressive by
making the person feel insecure, anxious, and threatened.
The way we use our voice, called *paralinguistics* in
communication theory, is a particularly powerful way of
affecting people. We should not underestimate the frequency
of nonverbally aggressive messages. These are sometimes
more common than verbal messages because less effort and
courage is required to give a look of exaggerated disbelief, for
example, than to say, "You must be crazy to believe that."

The nonverbal channels are also highly effective in
reinforcing verbal messages of aggression, thus heightening
their impact. For instance, an insult about physical
appearance ("You look absolutely disgusting and revolting
today.") could be reinforced by manipulating vocal
characteristics (e.g., by slowing the vocal rate for "disgusting"
and "revolting" and emphasizing the second syllable of both
words) and facial expression (e.g., a look of disgust).

What effects do these messages have on people? There
appear to be several.

Damaged Self-concepts
Hurt Feelings
Anger
Irritation
Embarrassment
Relationship Deterioration
Relationship Termination
Physical Violence

The first is the most fundamental effect of verbal aggression. Damage to one's self-concept can be even more harmful than physical aggression. A person could recover from a broken nose in approximately one month. If a disparaging remark is made about a child's nose (e.g., "Your nose looks like an eagle's beak"), the effect can endure for a lifetime.

The next four in the typology are more temporary. They occur for awhile but then tend to be forgotten. Much of the verbal aggression which occurs probably produces these more transitory feelings. Of course, these feelings sometimes lead to more serious consequences such as physical violence. Thus, we cannot excuse the more temporary effects as unimportant or trivial.

The next two have to do with interpersonal relationship effects. When verbal aggression is introduced into a relationship, that is a sign the relationship may be in a state of change or decay. The use of verbal aggression indicates that there is a desire to inflict psychological pain, and such an ingredient is not compatible with the notion of a healthy relationship.

Although the first seven effects are all serious to varying degrees, the most grave in terms of the individual and society is that verbal aggression sometimes leads to physical violence. Studies of violence in families (Gelles, 1974) and interviews with violent criminals (Toch, 1969) all reveal that violence usually is preceded by verbal aggression. One insult leads to another with increasing intensity until the pressure mounts to the point where rage explodes into physical violence.

Personal relationships are not the only place we find verbal aggression. Politicians regularly resort to personal attack. Baseball managers, in front of large crowds, impute that umpires have a variety of shortcomings, not excluding proper parentage. Minority groups are common targets for people who delight in personal attacks. Companies and organizations, at times, attempt destruction of one another's self-concept. Labor and management have shown remarkable endurance for being verbally aggressive throughout the duration of long strikes. On a global level, countries resort to verbal aggression even though it is entirely inappropriate in such places as the United Nations.

Verbal aggression appears to be a symbolic form of physical aggression. When we deliver a verbal blow to another person's self-concept we may in essence be saying, "Although I would like to be physically aggressive with you, I choose not to at this time, and instead I am delivering this verbal blow with hopes that it does some damage."

It is probably accurate to conclude that a good deal of the conflict, hostility, hate, and distrust in the world is stimulated by verbal aggression. If we could somehow eliminate verbal aggression from human interaction, the quality of life certainly would improve.

Scourges such as polio and smallpox have been almost completely eliminated. There is even hope that scientists will free us from the threat of cancer. Should we have a similar optimism about ridding ourselves of the destructiveness of verbal aggression?

That remains an open question. A pessimistic view would be that people are inherently violent, and verbal aggression is a natural symbolic consequence of that aspect of human nature. After all, it could be said, using words is better than using guns. However, a more optimistic assessment is plausible. Destructive forms of behavior, whether inherent or not, will in fact be avoided if people have alternative forms of behavior which are constructive and produce more personal satisfaction.

Even if it is not possible to eliminate verbal aggression on a large scale, you can control it on a small scale within your personal sphere of experience, your social universe. This book is designed to show you how arguing constructively can reduce greatly the amount of verbal aggression which you experience. The methods of argument which I shall present will discourage you from resorting to verbal aggression and will provide you with ways of controlling other people who try to be verbally aggressive with you.

Why Verbal Aggression?

In order to control verbal aggression, we need to understand why it occurs. There are at least four causes (Infante, 1987).

Psychopathology
Disdain
Social Learning
Argumentative Skill Deficiency

Psychopathology is a mental disorder. An example of a malfunction which could produce verbally aggressive behavior would be repressed hostility. At an early age, a person might have been a victim of prejudice and have been deeply hurt. The person may have been too young to retaliate and thus suppressed the felt hostility. Years later, the person may vent this repressed hostility by verbally attacking people who at least vaguely remind him or her of the original source of hurt.

Clinical intervention is the best way to correct such mental disorders. We will not attempt to deal with the problem in this book. Since a relatively small portion of the population suffers from psychopathologies, we cannot blame much of the verbal aggression which exists in society on mental illness. In fact, it may be rather unlikely that you have even been the victim of verbal aggression which was caused by genuine psychopathology.

The second cause is more prevalent. People use verbal aggression because they feel disdain for one another. Why people hate one another and what can be done about it also is beyond the scope of this book. However, I would like to suggest that we are not actually ignoring a major cause of verbal aggression. Probably, all of us have been the victim of a verbal attack by someone who disliked us greatly. Such experiences are not frequent for most people. We normally avoid interacting with people we dislike greatly. At times we must talk with such people, and that is when verbal aggression is likely. While memorable, these are usually rare events and do not constitute the bulk of the verbal aggression which we experience.

A social learning explanation for verbal aggression posits that verbally aggressive behavior is shaped by sources in society which use rewards and punishments. Sex differences are frequently explained in this light. Males are generally more verbally aggressive when compared to females. According to the social learning explanation, this is because society has taught males to be competitive, forceful, dominant, and aggressive. Females have been encouraged to be more submissive, less assertive, nice, and nonaggressive. Thus, females would tend to avoid verbal aggression more than males because it is not compatible with sex-role expectations. That is, verbal aggression is sanctioned less for females than males because it is not "ladylike."

The fourth cause has grown out of my research over the past several years. This explanation posits that when communication in a situation turns to a topic where you and at least one other person express conflicting positions, each individual adopts an "attack-and-defend" orientation. That is, your attention is focused primarily on two tasks, attacking the position which the other person has taken and defending your own position. If you are not skilled in the art of argument, you soon run out of things to say in defense of your position. While the urge to defend remains strong, you lack the resources to satisfy the need. So, you set up a defense around the next closest thing to your position on the issue—yourself. Thus, when your opponent says something against your position, you interpret this as an attack against you personally. That is, you mistake a genuine argument for verbal aggression; you "take it very personally." This may provoke you to be verbally aggressive toward your opponent, because you think he or she deserves it. If your opponent reciprocates this use of verbal aggression, a verbal fight could begin. Both individuals would believe the other person "fired the first shot."

The need to attack is similarly corrupted. If you are not a skillful arguer, you will soon exhaust what you have to say against your opponent's position. However, the need to attack still remains. Remember, this is a conflict situation. When it is your turn to speak, you must do something. You cannot stand there with your mouth open and no words pouring forth. So, if unable to attack your opponent's position, you tend to redirect your attack at the next closest target—your opponent.

Thus, lacking skill in arguing brings out "the worst in us" in emotionally charged conflict situations. Often we feel bad after attacking another person's self-concept. However, we also feel we were compelled to do so, that we had little choice. If you have not developed skill in arguing, you have little choice besides verbal aggression in satisfying the very powerful attack and defend needs which you feel in argumentative situations.

If the parties in an argument are skillful arguers, verbal aggression is less likely. Skillful arguers will rarely run out of things to say when defending and attacking positions. In fact, they typically think of so many things to say that the do not have enough time to reach their final thought on the controversial issue. Verbal aggression is also less likely because skillful arguers have a clear conception of the difference between genuine argument and verbal aggression (Rancer, Baukus, & Infante, 1985). They understand the destructiveness of verbal aggression and have methods for controlling it if it occurs.

Of course, we are not claiming highly skilled arguers never attack the self-concept of an opponent. Even proficient arguers lose their tempers, or they find themselves in discussions with people they dislike greatly and cannot resist the urge to voice that dislike. This aside, we are maintaining that acquiring skill in argumentation significantly reduces the chance that an individual will resort to verbal aggression in argumentative situations.

In terms of the available evidence, it would appear that social learning and an argumentative skill deficiency are two major causes of verbal aggression. Research does not indicate whether one of the two causes is more significant than the other. However, at least with the latter cause, it would appear something can be done. Deficiencies can be corrected. People can be taught to argue skillfully and constructively.

It would take unusual optimism to suppose that by teaching all children to argue constructively verbal aggression would be stamped out in a generation. However, it appears reasonable to speculate that such universal instruction would have a significant impact on the problem.

Mastering the concepts in this book will, at the very least, help you control verbal aggression in your world of experience. In addition, you will acquire communication skills which will enhance several aspects of your life. If enough people develop this preference for rational discourse, the effect could percolate upward and one day nations just might begin talking more rationally to one another. Politicians tend to talk the language of their constituents and will not use verbal aggression if it is abhorred by the electorate. It would be a safer and more pleasant world without verbal aggression.

Summary

Verbal aggressiveness is a facet of the hostility dimension of our personality and represents a very destructive tendency. Argumentation and verbal aggression are opposing forces when issues are discussed. One discourages the other. Types of constructive and destructive verbal clashes were examined in terms of the presence or absence of verbal aggression. The vantage points of the interactants, observers, and society were considered individually in assessing whether a message was verbally aggressive. A typology of eleven kinds of verbally aggressive messages was presented. The effects of verbal aggression were discussed from the most basic self-concept damage to physical violence. We speculated that reducing the amount of verbal aggression in society would have a favorable impact on the amount of violence in society. Encouraging constructive argument was seen as a way of controlling verbal aggression. Four causes were examined. Psychopathology and disdain were viewed as responsible for a relatively small portion of the verbal aggression in society. Social learning and an argumentative skill deficiency were seen as responsible for a greater portion of verbal aggression. Argumentative skill deficiency appears to be a major cause and also one that can be treated.

Exercises

1. Complete the Verbal Aggressiveness Scale which is in Appendix C at the end of the book.
2. Once you have completed the Verbal Aggressiveness Scale, turn to Appendix D. Compute your verbal aggressiveness

score according to the scoring instructions for the scale. Next, classify your score in terms of whether it is high, moderate, or low.

3. Administer the Verbal Aggressiveness Scale to a close friend, husband, or wife. Score the person's scale and classify the results. Compare the scores for the two of you. Is there a significant difference in the categories (e.g., one person high, the other moderate)? If there is a difference, what does it mean in terms of your relationship? Discuss verbal aggression in your relationship. Do the two of you agree on what constitutes verbal aggression in your relationship? What are the reasons for verbal aggression when it does occur? What could be done to prevent verbal aggression in your interpersonal relationship?

4. If you are enrolled in a class, divide into groups of about five persons each and discuss one or more of the following questions:

   a. How much of a problem is verbal aggression in your day-to-day interactions with other people?

   b. What are the most common types of verbally aggressive messages which you encounter?

   c. When you are verbally aggressive, what tends to be the reason(s)?

   d. Would you like to be more or less verbally aggressive? Why?

5. If you are not enrolled in a class, examine the questions in #4 by writing the answers in a notebook. Once you have completed this book, read your answers to see if you still hold the same views. It should be interesting to determine where and why changes have occurred.

Part II

Constructive Argumentation

3

Stating the Controversy in Propositional Form

In order to argue well, you must have a clear understanding of the controversy in a given situation (Freeley, 1966; Jensen, 1981). Stating the nature of the controversy in propositional form is an important first step. If you are arguing a topic with another person and you are unable to state the controversy in propositional form, then it could be concluded that the discussion has little direction, is not very meaningful, and there is little chance of a favorable outcome. In other words, you do not know exactly what you are talking about.

The first argumentative skill, then, has to do with gaining a clear understanding of the argumentative situation. From that base of understanding we can go on to argue well. Imagine what can happen when this skill is lacking. Suppose a husband and wife are arguing about money. The wife thinks the proposition being discussed is—"Resolved: That the wife in this family is irresponsible in her spending habits." The husband thinks the proposition is—"Resolved: That the husband in this family is not fulfilling his responsibility to provide for his family." It is easy to imagine such an argument turning into a bitter verbal fight. The reality is that both of them were probably wrong. The proposition they actually were arguing was—"Resolved: That major purchases and unnecessary minor purchases should be curtailed until this family is financially sound." If the husband and wife had discussed their concerns and recognized the true proposition, there probably would not have been an argument since both could have agreed with the stated proposition.

If the husband was not absolutely clear on what was being argued, it would have been a good idea for him to say something like, "What are we arguing here, that I am not fulfilling my responsibility to provide for my family?" (The word "Resolved" can be omitted since it is used mainly in formal debates and legislative settings.) In our example, the wife might have said, "No, we're not talking about that at all...." The outcome of the argument, then, would have been different.

Types of Propositions

Three types of propositions are common in argumentative situations (Mills, 1968; Wood, 1968):

Propositions of *Fact*
Propositions of *Value*
Propositions of *Policy*

Propositions of fact propose something that can be declared either true or false, existent or nonexistent. A proposition on nuclear arms control might be, "Russia has violated nearly every international agreement on limiting nuclear arms." A proposition of fact concerning our criminal justice system might be, "Relabilitation programs for convicted felons are ineffective." A married couple might argue the proposition, "We are financially able to buy a new car."

Propositions of fact can be concerned with either *past, present,* or *future* fact. For instance, we could argue whether something occurred in the past ("Many labor unions were run by mobsters."), or is happening now ("There is corruption in the Mayor's office."), or if something will happen in the future ("There will be gasoline shortages if we hinder off-shore oil exploration."). Finally, propositions of fact can be concerned with *definition.* Was an act one thing, or was it something else?

For instance, two propositions might be relevant in arguing about a soldier who ran from a battle: (1) "The soldier deserted"; (2) "The soldier retreated."

Propositions of value are concerned with whether something should be viewed favorably or unfavorably. Many of the issues which we argue are questions of value. "Abortions are wrong." "Legalized gambling is immoral." "Promotions in this company are unfair." "Our relationship is not worth the effort I have put into it." The basis for controversy when discussing propositions such as these is in the value systems of individuals. People often differ considerably in what they believe is right or wrong, good or bad, valuable or worthless, desirable or undesirable. When individuals apply their value standards to topics such as abortion or gambling, they can come up with very different conceptions of whether the thing is favorable or not. Such differences are the basis of argument.

Propositions of policy call for a change in policy: they propose some course of action. "A national lottery should be instituted." "The U.S. should permanently suspend military aid to Central America." "Our family should buy a new house." "You and I should take a study break by going out for a beer." Notice the word "Should" is used in policy propositions. It is assumed the particular action "could" be performed. If there is a question about that, a proposition of future fact would be needed for discussion, e.g., "The U.S. could become energy independent by the year 2000." Propositions of policy question whether the action should be taken.

When we talk with other people, many of the controversies which result have to do with action. "What should we do?" "Should we do this or that?" When someone proposes doing "this" instead of "that", a proposition has been made and the stage for an argument has been set.

As you can see, then, there are three different types of propositions in argument. However, in the next chapter I will contend that when we argue in favor of a proposition, whether it is fact, value, or policy, we are in essence making a proposal to those who oppose the proposition. Thus, we can think of arguments as *controversies over proposals*. This simplification will be important in terms of analyzing the propositions which we argue. Analysis (to be discussed in the next chapter) is a crucial part of the argumentative process. It is important to keep this part as *simple* and as *elegant* as possible.

The key idea in this part of the model of argumentative competence is that you should recognize propositions as they emerge in the course of communication. People will seldom if ever preface a proposition for argument with, "Resolved: That...." You must learn to recognize propositions by what the person claims. Did the individual claim something happened, is happening, or will happen? Did the person imply that something should be evaluated favorably or unfavorably? Did the person propose that an action should be taken?

Importance of Formulating Propositions

There are several reasons why stating the controversy in propositional form is important. First, this provides you with a way to determine whether you understand the controversy. You can easily verify your judgment by asking the other person, "Are you saying that...."

Second, by determining the proposition, you can assess the probable sides in the potential argument. Do you favor or oppose the proposition? How do the other relevant people align in terms of being pro or con? This will enable you to anticipate who the opposition would be if you decide to argue.

Third, stating the proposition provides a basis for deciding what material is relevant to the argument. If the proposition is — "Pornographic bookstores in our town should be abolished." — freedom of speech arguments and evidence about the effects of pornography would be relevant. Information about the private lives of pornographic film stars probably would not be relevant.

Finally, the statement of the proposition determines who has the *burden of proof* and who has the *benefit of presumption*. These are two important concepts and you should always determine whether you have the burden of proof or the benefit of presumption in an argument. Further, you want to make sure your opponents know which they have. As you will see, this will make a real difference in what you have to do in an argument.

The burden of proof means it is the obligation of the person who *affirms* the proposition to prove his or her case. We will call the side which favors the proposition the *affirmative*. Whether the proposition is one of fact, value, or policy, the person or persons who argue for the truth of the proposition have the burden of proof. In a court of law the proposition might be, "John Doe is guilty of armed robbery." The burden of proof is on the prosecutor. The defense does not have the burden of proving the accused is innocent. The defense has the burden of refutation in answer to the prosecution's arguments.

The benefit of presumption means the *status quo* (present system or present state of affairs) is favored. In a court of law, one is innocent until proven guilty. Innocence here is the *status quo*. The *status quo* is not changed unless there is good reason to change. Thus, the affirmative, those that favor the proposition, have the burden of proving that the *status quo* should be changed.

The propositions which we argue are controversial. Those who support the controversial statement, the affirmative, have the burden of proof. Those who oppose the proposition will be called the *negative*. They favor the *status quo*. Thus, the negative has the benefit of presumption. For instance if the proposition is— "Our company should use a lie detector test as a screening device for all job applicants."—those who are affirmative have the burden of showing there is a problem and that their proposal best solves the problem. The negative has the benefit of presumption. In this case, it means the current method of screening job applicants is assumed adequate unless it can be proven otherwise.

It is important that you do not take on the burden of proof unless you have to. If you are the negative on a proposition, do not allow the affirmative to pass the burden of proof to you. This is a common mistake made by unskilled arguers. In the previous example, the affirmative might say to the negative, "The way we screen applicants is so lacking it doesn't even deserve attention. Can you give us any reason why we should not change it?" If something like this happens to you, do not allow the attempt to shift the burden of proof. Instead, respond with something like, "Well, whether or not you want to give our current system any attention I think you have to since you said it is lacking. You can't ask me to defend something that has not even been attacked. You tell me what's wrong with the way we screen applicants and I will discuss your concerns."

In summary, recognize when an argumentative proposition emerges in communication situations. State it. Determine who the affirmative would be and who would be negative. Decide who would have the burden of proof and who would have the benefit of presumption. This will help you decide whether or not to argue.

Preparation for Arguing Propositions

When you argue a proposition for the first time, there seldom is a chance to research the topic before arguing. A typical condition while arguing is the need for more information; you very probably will think, "I wish I knew more about this." Of course, research is a vital part of formal debating. However, this book is about informal arguing. The arguments which we have in our everyday encounters with people are usually spontaneous. Thus, we might conclude that a research phase is practically irrelevent to arguing in interpersonal communication situations.

I would like to contend that there is a preparation phase for informal argument which is very important in terms of success. It may not be as highly structured as the procedure for formal debate which requires extensive library study using reference works, computer searches, and card catalogs to find a variety of articles, books, documents, and papers. Interviews are often conducted. The results of all of this research are recorded, copied, paraphrased, and filed for future use in an orderly, highly systematic manner. The preparation phase for informal argument is not as extensive as this but is nonetheless essential.

Preparation for informal argument might take one of two forms. First, you can develop information-seeking habits which will provide a versatile background of knowledge from which you can draw when you must argue propositions for the first time. We will discuss some activities which will insure that you will nearly always have something to say which is reasonably informed. Second, we usually argue propositions more than once. In fact, we argue some topics intermittently with various persons over a period of years. Thus, we need additional information about a specific proposition. If we do not continue to learn more about the issue, we may not do as well in a series of arguments if our opponent has improved his or her knowledge of the topic. Research on arguing indicates that arguing leads to learning because an argument stimulates our curiosity about the topics argued (Johnson and Johnson, 1979). After your first argument on a proposition, you probably feel a need to learn more. You become "information sensitive" to the given topic and thus pay attention to pertinent articles, news stories, etc. If you want to be extremely well prepared for a possible future argument, the research methods of formal debating are not irrelevant. If you are interested in learning more about how to do research for a formal debate, you should consult an argumentation and debate textbook (e.g., Freeley, 1966; Jensen, 1981; Mills, 1968; Windes & Hastings, 1965; Wood, 1968; Ziegelmuller & Dause, 1975).

In order to be prepared for arguments, to sound informed when you talk, it is necessary to develop and cultivate a *desire to be informed.* You should want to have information on a wide variety of topics which could be controversial in the course of your day-to-day activities. Having a desire to be informed means constantly being sensitive to information which may be useful someday. An analogy would be a garage sale shopper whose home is amply stocked with a multitude of items. If the toaster should break, there would be three more in the basement. Any eventuality would be covered. While perhaps not as ubiquitous as garage sales, the information we need for argument is readily available. Four common sources are: personal experience, talking with other people, the electronic media, the print media.

Your personal experience with a topic of argument is a valuable source of information. In fact, some research on persuasion has found that a person's *unique personal experience* is a powerful form of proof to support your position (Ostermeier, 1967; Wheeless, 1973). We are usually regarded as more expert on a topic if we have had some firsthand experience with it. Do not ignore yourself as a potential source of information for an argument. Pay close attention to your experiences and mentally rehearse what you would say about them. This planning will be highly beneficial when you cite the event to substantiate an argument. Be careful not to appear boastful when highlighting a personal situation in an argument. Such a perception will cancel the effectiveness of unique personal experience as a form of support for your arguments. An example of an argument using personal experience would be, "The security force in this airport is too lax. No one even looked at the screen when bags went through the x-ray machine, and they allowed a person, who said he was late, to go to the boarding area without first going through the metal detector."

Talking with other people is also a valuable source of information. When you talk with someone who has had a unique personal experience, think about where this information might be useful and mentally rehearse how you could use the event to illustrate the soundness of a particular proposition. This type of information is called *testimony* and is very useful in arguments, especially when your opponent and observers view the person you are referring to as highly credible. An example of an argument using the experience of others would be, "One of the reasons abortions should be outlawed is that they do severe psychological harm to the woman. I have a close friend who had an abortion and it has caused some real problems for her. She told me she has periods of depression, insomnia, and suffers from anxiety much of the time."

The electronic media, especially radio, television, and film, is a third source of information. You probably are exposed to at least one of these forms every day. Make the most of this because the electronic media can provide you with a wealth of information. Paying attention to the news on your car radio is a good place to begin. All too often, we change the station in search of more music when the news begins. One of the best ways of becoming interested in the news is to have it structured into your day. Make the local and national television news programs a regular part of your morning and evening activities. When you hear stories of particular interest, mentally rehearse what you would say about the issue. Practice pronunciation of names so that you do not stumble when you try to use the name in an argument. This is embarrassing and frustrating when it happens but it can usually be avoided by repeating a difficult name several times when you first hear it. Films also are a good source of ideas. Many films carry a message about current issues and the human condition in general. Determine what that message is and try to remember it.

Finally, one of the richest sources of information is the print media, especially books and periodicals. If you love to read, you probably do not need the exhortation I am about to deliver. If you want to improve your arguing, read more. Of course, there is more to improving your argumentative behavior than simply reading more. However, it is a good place to begin. With more breadth and depth of knowledge, it will be easier for you to do the things discussed in the following chapters: invent arguments, present arguments, refute the arguments that other people present. There are several reading habits that facilitate effective arguing.

It is a good idea to read a newspaper thoroughly every day. This is one of the best ways of keeping informed about current events which may become the subjects of arguments. However, many of the topics which we argue are more personal. "Where should we cut living expenses?" would be one example. Newspapers also provide information about such personal topics and can be very useful when arguing those ideas. The typical daily newspaper provides a satisfying range of stories. If you take the time to read the entire paper daily, you will be well on your way to being at least minimally prepared on many of the topics which you argue.

A second area is periodicals. There are several good weekly news magazines. You should try to read at least one of them weekly. Three of the best known are *Time*, *Newsweek*, and *U.S. News and World Report*. As with newspapers, these publications carry a variety of stories in areas such as science, medicine, music, and religion which will provide you with a good assortment of material for arguments. There also are many specialized periodicals. In what area or areas are you most interested? Probably many of the propositions that you argue will be in such areas. Periodicals in your area of interest should be read. They contain some of the most current information and can be very helpful in arguments. For instance, if you are interested in physical fitness, read a physical fitness magazine such as *Sports Fitness* at least once a month.

The library is another source of information. A library is a rich storehouse for an amazing amount and variety of information. Do you know how to use a library? If not, you can learn easily. The library is an important part of the "desire to be informed" attitude which we discussed earlier. We will not instruct you here in how to use the library for argument preparation. You can obtain that direction from the argumentation textbooks cited earlier.

Summary

The first portion of the model of argumentative competence involves stating the nature of a controversy in propositional form. This skill pertains to achieving a clear understanding of the argumentative situation and serves to avoid misunderstandings. Definition of the controversy is facilitated and the parties are able to "agree upon what to disagree." Three types of propositions were discussed: fact, value, policy. Each is important in both formal and informal argument. Four reasons for formulating propositions were presented. A special emphasis was placed on the fourth which pertained to determining the burden of proof and the benefit of presumption. The positions of affirmative and negative on a proposition also were explained. These ideas depend upon determination of what is the status quo. Knowing when to assume and when to refuse the burden of proof is an important facet of the first portion of the argumentative competence model. The preparation phase for arguing propositions was discussed. The emphasis was on preparing for informal arguments. Four sources of information were examined: personal experience, testimony of others, the electronic media, the print media.

Exercises

1. Keep a log of the topics which you argue for the next week. State what the proposition was for each argument. Classify each proposition in terms of fact, value, or policy. For each argument, did you have the burden of proof or the benefit of presumption?

2. Write a 500 word essay which analyzes the data gathered in #1. Arrive at some conclusions in terms of what the data say about your argumentative behavior.

3. Prepare a three minute speech on the data gathered in #1. State conclusions in terms of what the data say about your argumentative behavior.

4. Practice formulating propositions. For each of the topics listed, write a proposition of fact, one of value, and one of policy.

   Labor Unions
   Legalized Abortions
   Televised Violence
   Pornography
   Lie Detectors
   Gun Control
   U.S. Foreign Military Aid
   Nuclear Arms Control
   Wiretapping
   Religious Cults
   Driving while Intoxicated
   Divorce
   Freedom of Speech

5. Write a 500 word essay or prepare a four minute speech which assesses how you prepare yourself for possible communication about controversial topics. How do you get information? What do you do with it? Do you use mental rehearsal? How?

6. Determine at least two ways that you can improve your preparation to discuss controversial issues. State these as goals on a piece of paper. Place the paper in a place where you will see it regularly. Make these changes over a period of the next several weeks.

4

Inventing Arguments

One of our central ideas is that to argue well you must have available a variety of good arguments. The person who is unskilled at argument typically reports a deficiency: "When I'm in an argumentative situation I can't think of what to say." Or, it is claimed: "I feel like my mind is frozen during an argument; the thaw comes later, when I'm by myself; then I think of some real good points."

A common misconception is that the ability to discover arguments—knowing what to say—is a genetic trait. The common belief is: "Either you've got it, or you don't. If you don't, there's nothing you can do about it." This is a misconception because you *can* be taught the process which the ancient Greek and Roman communication theorists called *inventio*. This process involves inventing arguments. Research indicates people can be taught the process of invention; they will then be able to discover more arguments, be better consumers of communication, and be perceived more favorably when they argue with other people (Infante, 1971a; Infante & Grimmett, 1971).

A basic idea for this second step in learning how to argue is that inventing arguments results from a systematic analysis of the proposition being argued. Once you (1) state the controversy in propositional form you (2) then analyze it in order to discover what to say. How do you analyze a proposition? There are numerous systems of analysis which

45

have been developed over the long history of communication theory. I am going to present one which is extremely useful for a wide variety of the propositions which we commonly argue. The system may be used whenever someone argues that we should do something or take a proposed course of action. This can include all three types of propositions which we discussed earlier: fact, value, policy. We can think of these as *proposals* that one person makes to another: heroin should be legalized; we should buy something; we should work longer hours; we should favor the idea that vitamin C prevents the common cold; we should value opera as one of the highest forms of art.

The first three examples were propositions of policy, the fourth was fact, and the fifth was value. These are all proposals because in each case the person who favors the proposition (the affirmative) is proposing that those who oppose the proposition (the negative) should do something. A particular course of action is implied. For instance, in the vitamin C example, the proposition of fact is actually, "Resolved: That vitamin C prevents the common cold." However, I am contending that the person who argues for the proposition is actually proposing to opponents that they should favor the idea that vitamin C prevents colds and behave accordingly. The same could be maintained for propositions of value. In the fifth example above, the affirmative would propose that those who are negative toward the proposition should incorporate the idea — that opera is one of the highest forms of arts — into their values and hence lifestyles.

Viewing most, if not all, of the propositions which we argue as proposals enables us to use an inventional system for proposals. Otherwise, we would need separate systems for propositions of fact, value, and policy. As in science, I believe the law of parsimony should prevail — favor the least complex, the most straightforward approach.

Another reason for viewing arguments as controversies over proposals is that it alerts us to the reality that when someone argues with us they really want us to follow a particular course of action. This is true even when the argument seemingly is over a question of fact such as whether something happened. For instance, if a wife argues that her husband was drunk at a party the night before, an implied course of action in the argument might be that the wife is advocating that the husband drink less and behave in a less embarrassing manner at parties.

The system for inventing arguments about proposals which I shall now explain is not only well tested in terms of classroom use, but also, as discussed earlier, has yielded very favorable results in experimental research (for research on a different but related system see Nelson, 1970). The system is presented in Table 1.

The first thing you need to do is to memorize the Inventional System. If you are going to use it, you need to have the system available when you need it. Thus, I can find no suitable substitute for memorization.

Table 1

The Inventional System

Major Issues and Sub-Issues

1. Problem

    a. What are the signs of a problem?
    b. What is the specific harm?
    c. How widespread is the harm?

2. Blame

    a. What causes the problem?
    b. Is the present system at fault?
    c. Should the present system be changed?

3. Solution

    a. What are the possible solutions?
    b. Which solution best solves the problem?

4. Consequences

    a. What good outcomes will result from the solution?
    b. What bad outcomes will result from the solution?

As you are working to memorize the Inventional System you may begin to realize some things about it. For instance, the major issues and their sub-issues are general, so much in fact that they can be applied to nearly any topic or proposal. With training, this system will enable you to have something relevant, and hopefully intelligent, to say on most of the topics you ever encounter. The questions focus around the idea of problem-solution. Most of the proposals which we argue fit the problem-solution mold. Finally, you might realize the span of questions is indeed broad. If you are able to answer all of these questions for a given proposal which is being argued, you can have some confidence that you have reasonably covered the topic. This is something we are concerned with when we discuss a controversial topic. Are we missing something? A good system of analysis reduces the chance that you will miss something of importance.

Using the Inventional System

Let us now examine the Inventional System to see how it can be used. We will consider two ways: how to use the system when you are proposing a course of action (when you are affirmative on the proposition); how to use the system when you are against a proposal (when you are negative on the proposition).

If you are proposing something, you are calling for a change in the status quo; the present system operates in the absence of what you want. If you try to get someone to work harder, the status quo is how hard the person presently works. Proposing a change in the status quo means you have the *burden of proof* to show that the status quo should be changed and that your direction of change is best. That is, you have to show there is a *need for what is being proposed* and that your *proposal will satisfy the need.* Remember the concepts "need" and "proposal will satisfy the need." These two concepts will be the major points you will advocate when you argue in favor of a proposal. When you argue against a proposal these two concepts will be the core of your attack. You will contend that those who favor the proposal have not established that there is a need for the proposal and further, even if there was a need, the proposal would not satisfy the need.

Examine the Inventional System. You will see it is based on the two concepts of showing there is a need to change the status quo and that the proposal will satisfy the need. The first two major issues—Problem and Blame—and their respective sub-issues are concerned with the need for the proposal. The Solution and Consequences issues are focused on showing the proposal will satisfy the need. How would you use these issues to invent arguments? Remember, these are possible issues in an argument. All may not be relevant or necessary for a particular argument.

For example, suppose you are arguing for the proposition, "That your good friend Sue should change jobs." Your friend opposes the proposition. Recall also that according to our reasoning you are making a proposal. You are proposing to your friend that she change jobs. Use the potential issues in the Inventional System as a guide to what you can argue.

For the Problem part of the need for a change, examine your friend's status quo (present situation) in terms of the "signs of a problem" sub-issue. You might think of the following: "Sue, I think you should give some thought to sending out resumes to other companies. I can see some indications (i.e., signs) that things are not right in your present job. You got passed over for a promotion to that newly created position in PR. Your boss is not able to recognize quality writing such as yours. Your salary is not as high as it should be. And, also, you seem nervous and upset when you get home from work." For the "specific harm" sub-issue you might determine these arguments: "Your company is a mediocre PR firm that can't figure out how to use your talents. This can hurt your career because if you stay too long it seems like you can't make it in a mediocre company. Besides hurting your career, I think this job can hurt you psychologically. They aren't providing the support and positive environment you need to be happy as you grow professionally."

When we consider the "widespread" sub-issue, we might decide it is not needed for this argument. Recall, we do not have to use all of the issues for every argument. Frequently, this would be a valuable issue to use in formulating arguments.

If we were arguing for legalized heroin, we could maintain that a high percentage of robberies are committed to support heroin habits. Such an argument would have to do with the issue of "How widespread is the harm?"

Based on the three sub-issues to the major issue of Blame, you might say, "I believe the major reason for your problems with this company is sexual discrimination (first sub-issue). Your firm has held you back because you are a woman. They have moved men ahead of you in rank and salary who were not as qualified (second sub-issue). I don't think you should expect this is going to change. None of your superiors will retire for a long time, and don't bet on a male chauvinist changing (third sub-issue)."

For the Solution portion of an argument, there are two sub-issues. If you propose only one solution, then the second sub-issue actually involves explaining how your solution will solve the problem. In our example, something like the following might be said: "Sue, I think you should start job hunting. Send out resumes. Contact PR firms with openings. Maybe join a placement service. Since you now know the field, only talk with firms that are known not to discriminate."

You could argue the Consequences issue like this: "If you move to a less chauvinistic company, I feel confident your talents will be recognized, you will make much more money in the long run, and more importantly, you will have peace of mind." You might decide there is not much to say about possible bad outcomes, the second sub-issue.

This example has illustrated how the Inventional System is used when you present a proposal to another person. What was done here, essentially, was we "told" ourselves, "say something persuasive about the problem," then, "say something convincing about blame," etc. We really are "coaching" ourselves. Research (Infante, 1971a; Nelson, 1970) indicates that such coaching increases the quantity of our arguments. Recent research suggests the quality of the arguments also is enhanced (Infante, 1981, 1985). Of course, if you ask yourself the questions about problem, blame, etc., and you come up with nothing or little to say, you have demonstrated to yourself that you have little basis for arguing. In that case, heed your analysis. Do not argue. However, you probably will discover that once you learn how to stimulate your analytical abilities with the questions from the Inventional System, you usually will create arguments that can be used. As maintained in Chapter 1, we should not argue excessively since too much of anything, even a good thing, can be disruptive. Therefore, just because we create arguments does not mean that we should always use them.

Now we will examine how to use the system to invent arguments when someone presents a proposal to you. The basic strategy is to analyze what the person says in terms of the Inventional System to determine three things: (1) which of the four major issues and sub-issues did the person ignore; (2) was enough said about the issues which were discussed; (3) do you agree with what was said for each of the issues addressed?

The first two have to do with what the person did not say. Once you determine which issues the person ignored, you can argue that the adversary has an obligation to establish those points. For example, if a person advocates legalizing casino gambling in the State of New York and emphasizes the good consequences, you could press the person on Problem and Blame. You could say, "What's wrong with the way things are now? Who is being harmed by the current gambling policies? Just how great is this harm?"

For the second point, when you feel not enough was said on an issue, you could challenge your opponent in the following manner: "You said our current gambling policy in New York is deficient because it encourages organized crime. Are you saying everyone in New York is becoming a member of organized crime, or are you saying one person is, or something in between? I think you need to clarify that conclusion." Usually, you can come up with an argument when you realize the person did not say enough about an issue (in this example it was the "widespread" sub-issue).

For the third point, you determine whether you agree with what was said for the issues addressed. Where you disagree will be the basis for direct clash with your opponent. For the previous two points the arguments were more indirect; they were actually challenges for the opponent to say more. More direct clash involves questioning particular evidence and/or reasoning. For instance, if an opponent says, "Legalizing casino gambling will benefit education greatly in terms of increased revenues," you might say, "The past performance of legalized casino gambling in improving educational finances has not been especially good. The educational systems of Nevada and New Jersey did not change much due to gambling revenues." This more direct opposition is a very exciting part of arguing and will be covered more thoroughly in Chapter 6 which deals with attacking other positions.

Features of the Inventional System

There are several aspects of the Inventional System which should be emphasized. First, you may have wondered, how is this set of questions a system of invention? Does it really cause something to be invented? The knowledge that our minds are more productive when stimulated systematically has existed since the time of Ancient Greece. The Inventional System is a set of questions designed to prompt your mind methodically in all communication situations where one person makes a proposal to another person. By asking yourself questions such as "what is the specific harm relevant to this proposal?" you are forcing yourself to deal with the proposal in a particular way. Because you ask the question, you probably will come up with an answer. The question induces a response which might otherwise have been undiscovered. Research conducted with the Inventional System supports this idea. People using the inventional system discovered arguments which other people did not realize (Infante, 1971a).

Second, although the scope of the ten sub-issues is indeed broad, there are other possible sub-issues. For instance, a potential issue under Problem could be; "Can the *status quo* solve the problem?" If it can be shown that the present system can get rid of the harm, then why throw it out for a new, untried system? An issue under Consequences might be "What is the ratio of good to bad consequences?" This suggests that the more the good consequences outweigh the bad, the better the proposal. It is clear, then, that the Inventional System does not cover everything. However, it covers enough; it stimulates you to a level where you can be as comprehensive as is necessary in the situation. We could include many more sub-issues in the system. If we did that, there would be a danger that it would become too cumbersome, too complex, and too awkward. Too much brevity renders a system virtually useless; too much length becomes unmanageable. In its present state, the Inventional System with ten questions is a compromise between being too brief or too long.

Third, the Inventional System is both rigid and flexible. That is, it specifies four major issues when a proposal is made in a communication situation: problem, blame, solution, consequences. Each of the four areas has sub-issues. However, it is not always necessary to talk about each issue and sub-issue. For instance, both parties in an argument might have a clear understanding of the Problem and thus that area need not be discussed. The argument would go immediately to Blame and then Solution. Sometimes the consequences of a solution may be so obvious that little attention is necessary to this facet of the proposal.

Fourth, mastering the Inventional System probably will have a pervasive and enduring effect on your thinking. You will analyze proposals which you and other people make in terms of the four issues and their sub-issues. Thus, your first reaction to the proposal that you should buy a new car might be: "Is there really a need for this?" Your mind will then run through the sub-issues pertaining to "signs," "harm," and "how widespread." When this happens you will have acquired a *critical thinking mind-set*. This is a highly valued way of thinking and is characterized by systematic and thorough analysis while utilizing rigorous standards to determine the worth of an idea.

Fifth, and finally, although the Inventional System may be used to produce substance which can be employed in an argument, it does have other uses. You can use it to help you decide whether or not to argue. If you have a proposal you are thinking of making to another person, you might analyze it with the Inventional System and decide "I really don't have much of a need case (problem and blame) so I better not speak up until I do." Or, you might listen to another person present a case for a proposal and decide the four major issues were covered so well that it would not make much sense to argue. You can also use the Inventional System to analyze any kind of persuasive message, even when you do not have a chance to argue with another person (e.g., a commercial on television).

The purpose of this chapter was to provide you with a workable system for discovering arguments in order to advocate a proposal or to attack a proposal. Once you have arguments, a concern is how to present and defend them. That is the focus of the next chapter. We will examine refutation in Chapter 6. Refutation involves attacking others' arguments and is one of the most exciting as well as challenging parts of argumentation.

Summary

Invention is one of the most important parts of argumentation theory. The Inventional System taught in this chapter is designed for use when advocating or opposing a proposal. Propositions of policy, fact, and value can all be viewed as the affirmative making a proposal to the negative. This conception was adopted to achieve the goal of parsimony in the inventional process. The Inventional System has four major issues: problem, blame, solution, consequences. Each major issue has two or three sub-issues. The issues deal with whether there is a need to change the status quo and whether the proposal will satisfy the need. Use of the system was explained for advocating a proposal and for opposing a proposal. Research suggests that the Inventional System does stimulate individuals to discover arguments that would not have been thought of otherwise. Several features of the Inventional System were discussed. The system stimulates thinking about controversy, alters the way you think about proposals, and provides guidance for when to argue and when not to argue.

Exercises

1. Use the Inventional System to analyze a newspaper editorial. What major issues did the writer attempt to cover? Which sub-issues were discussed? Were issues presented which are not in the Inventional System? Which issues, that were not covered, should have been discussed? Why? Of the issues dealt with, which were argued most convincingly? Which were least convincing?

2. Use the Inventional System to analyze an ad in a magazine. What proposal is advocated? Which of the major issues were addressed in order to advocate the proposal? Which issues were not addressed? Was the persuasion attempt hurt by the omission? If you could speak to the ad makers and demand that they tell you more, what would you say?

3. Select ads which you think do a particularly good job of addressing one or more of the major issues. Explain the reasons for your assessments.

4. Use the Inventional System as a guide to interview someone who advocates a particular course of action. The person could be a prominent member of your community or an "average" person. Ask the person about each of the four major issues and as many of the sub-issues as necessary. Write a report of the interview. How well did Inventional System function in enabling you to analyze the proposal?

5. What is a proposal that you have advocated recently in an argument? Using the Inventional System as a guide, interview yourself on the proposal. If possible, tape record the interview. Listen to the interview. In what ways did the Inventional System stimulate you to think of ideas?

6. Prepare a three minute speech on what you would cover in a speech where you advocate a particular position on a controversial topic. Give an overview of what you would say for each major issue and each sub-issue. Be prepared to answer questions from the audience on your choices.

5

Presenting and Defending Your Position

Our attention in this chapter will focus on presenting and defending your position. This involves the presentation of a single argument and also the positions which you may take when supporting or opposing a proposal. Recall that this is the third part of argumentative competence. The first two parts were more concerned with preparing for an argument. This, and the next two chapters, will deal with how you should behave in an actual argument.

Presenting an Argument

We shall use a four-step procedure for presenting an argument. All four steps are not necessary for every argument. You must use your judgment, along with the principles in this chapter, to determine which steps are and are not needed for a particular argument.

1. State what you are claiming.
2. Present the evidence for your claim.
3. Present the reasons for your claim.
4. Summarize to show what you established.

In the first step, you specify precisely what you want others to accept. In argumentation theory, this is called the *claim* (see Toulmin, 1958). It is, basically, the conclusion of your argument. When you state what you are claiming, it is assumed that you are prepared to support the claim and also that you are willing to try to defend it. If not, there is no argument. A person who just states a claim such as, "Communists control the universities in this country," and does not offer support for the statement is practicing the emotional expression or self-disclosure of beliefs, not argumentation. You could also think of a claim as a *thesis*. This is a conclusion you reach after considering relevant reasoning and evidence.

The second step is especially important. Here you present the evidence for your claim. This represents part of the grounds for your claim. Evidence is the substance which bears on your claim. This could be a specific example, statistics, or testimony. To support the claim, "Johnny cannot be trusted with the family car," you might offer the examples that, "He has several citations for reckless driving and speeding." When you have more than one example you can summarize and characterize the data. You will then be using statistics, a very powerful type of evidence used to support claims. Averages, medians, group comparisons, etc. are all statistical tools which can be used to advantage. To support the claim, "that capital punishment is racially biased," statistics reported in a 1985 Associated Press article could be cited. The convicted killer of a white person has about one chance in nine of being executed while the killer of a black person has a chance of only one in twenty. Testimony involves quoting a source who has said something relevant to a claim. To support the claim, "we should cancel our picnic," you might quote the National Weather Service as having said there is nearly a 100% chance of rain.

In formal debate there is a good deal of opportunity to gather evidence. That is, a research phase is an important part of the argumentation process. Again, our focus here is not with formal debating but with informal arguing in our interpersonal relationships. As we explained in Chapter 3, the first time you argue a proposition you must get by with the evidence you already possess. However, developing a "desire to be informed" creates information-seeking habits which make it likely you will almost always have at least some relevant information. Once we argue a proposition, we usually become motivated to learn more about the topic so we will have more evidence the next time we argue.

The reasons for our claim which we give in step 3 represent our attempt to convince others that our claim is justified by our evidence. This is a particularly important part of presenting an argument. The evidence which we cite to support our claims sometimes is not so compelling that nothing more needs to be said. Argumentation theorists have discussed at least three types of reasons we can use for making our evidence-claim connection compelling. One type is *motivational*; the reasoning here is based on the other person's values, needs, and attitudes. Imagine you have advanced the claim, "We should go to our neighbor's garage sale," with this evidence: "The garage sale has a variety of inexpensive exercise equipment." The motivational reason could be, "You have wanted to begin a physical fitness program but could not afford the equipment." This would reinforce the relevancy of the evidence to the claim. The idea here is to try to increase motivation for agreeing with the claim. When arguing with other persons, try to determine their needs, the things they value, their attitudes. If you can show that what you are claiming is related to their values, needs, and attitudes, they will tend to believe you gave a "good reason" for your claim.

A second type of reason is *authoritative*. Here the reason for accepting the claim is based on the credibility of the source of our evidence. For the claim, "An active person like you should eat more complex carbohydrates," you might offer this evidence, "*Sports Medicine* said complex carbohydrates such as bread and potatoes are an important source of energy for active people." The authoritative reason could be expressed, "*Sports Medicine* is one of the most trusted publications for information pertaining to our health." When you know the source of your evidence, and you think it would help acceptance of your claim, mention that the credibility of the source leaves little room for doubting your evidence.

A third type of reason involves *expected relationships*. These take the form of "If this, then this." We argue that we have come to expect certain things and that our evidence-claim combination represents such a relationship. We might claim, "Russia will probably violate a proposed nuclear arms reduction agreement with the U.S.," and base the claim on the evidence that "Russia has violated 50 of 52 previous international agreements." Our reasoning is that "past violations are indications of future violations." This is an example of *classification:* what is true for the class (international agreements) is true of each individual (the particular nuclear arms agreement) in the class. An example of another type of relationship that we have come to expect is: "We should hire ChemLawn to spray our lawn with fertilizer and weed and bug control" (claim); "our neighbor's lawn is beautiful now that ChemLawn is doing their yard" (evidence); "our yard is so similar to theirs that if it worked for them, it also should work for us" (reason). This is called an *analogy;* if two things are similar, what is true for one should be true for the other. There are other types of expected relations such as generalization, sign, causation. However, our purpose is not to be overly complex with the various forms of reasons. Rather, we want you to realize the principle of "expected relationships" and to use such expectations when appropriate to give more emphasis to the validity of linking certain evidence with a claim.

The fourth step in presenting an argument (summarize to show what you established) is necessary especially when your argument is not brief. If your presentation has been at all lengthy, it is a good idea to summarize. This provides the listener with an additional opportunity to understand the implications of what you are saying, and the mere repetition of material sometimes increases the chance of acceptance.

In review, presenting a single argument involves four steps. Think of them as claim-evidence-reasons-summary. All of the steps are not necessary for every argument if there is a strong likelihood that the listener will think of the omitted steps without prompting. This is a highly desirable occurrence since it is generally believed that we are more convinced of something if we think of it ourselves. For instance, if you present the evidence of Russia's past violations of international agreements (our earlier example) it might be effective to omit the claim. Allow the listener to conclude that Russia probably will violate a proposed nuclear arms agreement. Thus, the four-step procedure for presenting an argument is flexible. However, be prepared for each step, even if you decide not to use it.

Now that we have covered how to present a single argument, we will examine how to present a group of related arguments — your *position* — on the proposition which you are arguing. We will discuss three basic positions which you may take in supporting a proposition. Then we will examine three positions which you may take in opposing a proposition.

Positions for Supporting a Proposition

The first position is the *Problem-Solution,* or *Need-Proposal* strategy which we discussed earlier. Your individual arguments can be arranged so that they illustrate a problem or a need for a proposal and that a proposed solution will satisfy the need. Use the same four-step procedure for presenting a single argument to present your position. If you are favoring a legalized heroin proposal, the "claim" step of your position could be, "I think there are serious shortcomings in the way we deal with heroin addiction and I believe a system of legalized heroin would solve those problems." The second and third steps would involve presenting individual arguments about problem and solution (remember, each of those arguments would follow the claim-evidence-reasons-summary model). The fourth step in presenting your position would be to summarize to show that you have established your entire case. This four-step plan also applies to the other types of positions which we will discuss below.

The second position for favoring a proposal is called the *Comparative-Advantages* strategy. The focus in this approach is not on the problem or need issues but on the proposal. The proposal will result in advantages or good consequences not produced by the status quo. The major contention is, "this plan will work, it will produce these advantages." The justification for the proposal is that it will provide more advantages than are being provided by the status quo. This can be a difficult position to defend if the opposition dwells on the Problem and Blame major issues. For instance, imagine you favor the proposal, "That this family should buy a new car." Your Comparative-Advantages case says this new car will provide advantages which do not exist with the status quo (current car): greater comfort, better handling, more style, excellent gas mileage. However, it will be difficult to have the argument center on those advantages if one of your family members insists upon the Problem and Blame issues: "What is wrong with our current car? How serious is each problem? Can't we fix the current car to solve the problems?" (Remember this strategy when someone wants to talk only about their proposal). You would respond that it is not a question of what is wrong with the current car but a discussion of which car would be more advantageous.

The third position which can be taken in arguing for a proposal is the *Ideal Solution*. For this stance, you would specify the criteria for an ideal solution to the particular problem or need being considered. Then you would proceed to argue that your solution or proposal best meets the criteria so it should be adopted. Let us say you favor the proposition, "That this family should go to New York City for this year's vacation." To support this proposal you say, "Our vacation should be to a place where there: (1) is something for everyone to do, (2) are a lot of places to eat, (3) are numerous theatres, (4) is good public transportation." In doing this you have set up the criteria for an "Ideal" solution to the need. You would then argue that New York City best matches those requirements. If a family member offers another alternative, you would take the criteria one at a time and argue that the alternative does not fulfill the criteria as well as New York City does.

Positions for Opposing a Proposition

We will cover three positions which may be taken in opposing a proposal. The first involves a complete *Denial* of the need for the proposal and denies that the proposal will satisfy the need. The opposition could be challenged on each of the major issues and sub-issues in the Inventional System. If this position is taken, it is important to keep the pressure on your opposition for all four major issues. In a sense, keep your opponent busy trying to put out one fire while you continue to ignite the other issues. No matter how well the adversary deals with some of the issues, it is usually possible to point out that other issues were not covered sufficiently. Because of the diversity and scope of the Inventional System, it is possible to put up a seemingly endless string of barriers for someone who proposes to change the status quo.

The Denial position is a highly effective strategy. However, in some circumstances it is not the best position to take. When complete denial of the problem or need is not possible the *Repairs* position is particularly effective. Essentially, with a Repairs position you agree that there are some things wrong, that the status quo has some problems. However, you maintain, we do not need some completely new system. If we make some improvements in the status quo, some repairs, the problems would be solved. In our earlier example of the Comparative-Advantages case for a new car, a Repairs position could contend that while comfort, handling, style, and gas mileage are deficient in the current car those problems could be corrected for about one-fifth the cost of a new car. One of the basic strategies with the Repairs position is that you depict your opponent's proposal as being extravagant, going overboard, calling for a large change when only some simple repairs are needed. This strategy tends to be very effective because humans usually are opposed to unnecessary change and are attracted to simple repairs which prolong the life of something which they would rather not have to change.

The third position for opposing a proposal is the *Counterplan*. This is used when you agree there are serious problems with the status quo and that it should be changed; however, you do not think your opponent's proposal is the best way to solve the problem. You offer a different plan to satisfy the need, a different approach for completely changing the status quo. Not much time in the argument is spent on the problem issue. Instead, the focus is on which solution, yours or the opponent's, best solves the problem. This means the consequences issue (the fourth major issue) is argued

extensively. To continue with our new car example, suppose
you agree with the problems of the status quo. While the other
person wants to buy a full-size luxury Oldsmobile, you offer the
counterplan of buying a sporty car, a Camaro. The argument
would then shift to which plan would have the most good
consequences and the fewest bad consequences; which car
would best satisfy the need.

Defending Your Position

In argumentation theory, *rebuttal* refers to the part of the
argumentative process where you attempt to rebuild your
position. The basic situation is that you have presented an
argument or set of arguments, your opponent has attempted to
refute what was said, and the attention has shifted back to you
to see if you can defend your position. It is obvious that this is
a most important part of an argument. If you show that your
position still stands, you have greatly increased the chance
that you will win the argument. To defend your position you
need to be able to rebuild the arguments which were attacked
by your opponent. To accomplish this we will follow a four-step
procedure for rebuilding an argument.

1. Summarize your original argument.
2. Review your opponent's refutation.
3. Present and support your objections to the attack.
4. Summarize your defense emphasizing the validity
   of your original position.

We will examine each step. For our example, imagine that
you presented an argument favoring the voucher system
proposal for education. Under this system the parents of each
student in a school district would be given a voucher for the
cost of educating a child in that district. Parents could choose
to send the child to the local public school, a private school, or
another public school. The school selected would receive the
voucher. One of your arguments was: "A voucher system for
education would provide freedom of choice for students
through high school. There is already freedom of choice after

high school. Why shouldn't freedom apply to younger students as well as college students?" In response to this, suppose an opponent of the proposal said: "One of your reasons for advocating a voucher system is that it will extend freedom of choice for school into the high school and elementary school. My main objection to this is that with such a system some neighborhood schools will get so few students they will literally have to go out of business. The popular schools will be over-crowded. New schools will be formed adding to the turmoil. So, I think this proposal will cause chaos in our public school systems and therefore should not be adopted."

When it is your turn to speak you could follow our four-step format for defense. The first step is usually quite brief. The major purpose is for you to specify exactly what you are defending. In our example you might say, "I maintained that a major reason for adopting the voucher system for education is that it would provide educational freedom of choice for all students."

The second step is also a brief summary. In this case review your adversary's attempted refutation: "You said a reason for not adopting the voucher system is that it would create chaos in our public school systems."

The third step is the actual defense step. It can involve several tactics.

1. Attack your opponent's evidence or lack of evidence.
2. Attack your opponent's reasoning.
3. Present additional evidence to support your point.
4. Present further reasoning.
5. Issue a counter attack.

How to attack evidence and reasoning, the first two tactics, will be explained in the next chapter; we will not attempt to cover them at this time. In our example, however, we will try to utilize all five tactics to some extent. Remember while you are studying the next chapter that the ways of attacking another person's evidence and reasoning all may be used when you are defending your position. You can attack the evidence and the reasoning the opponent used in attacking you.

Accordingly, we might say: "I would have to disagree with your argument about chaos for several reasons. You did not give even a hypothetical example of how this could happen. I don't think you can because it will not be chaos that will happen. What will be experienced will be the open market and free enterprise system extended into education. The good schools will prosper, the schools not providing what the public needs will go out of business. I just want to point out that the wealthy already enjoy the freedom of choice this proposal provides. They send their children to the schools of their choice. I would like you to answer why all people should not have this opportunity. This country is based on the ideas of free choice and equal opportunity for *all* people."

The fourth step in our rebuttal procedure is to summarize your defense briefly and emphasize the validity of your position. In our example, you could say: "So, I am saying that's not chaos you are referring to; that's beneficial change. There has been a lot of talk lately about improving the public schools. The voucher system is a way to do just that." You may not use this step for every argument you rebuild. But do use it at least some of the time because it reinforces the idea that your position stands. This step is part of an ancient communication formula which goes something like this: "Tell them what you are going to say; tell them; then tell them what you said." The major reason this simple notion has survived years of practice is that it does work.

Summary

This chapter dealt with presenting a position and then defending it once it has been attacked. A four-step procedure was taught for presenting an argument: claim-evidence-reasons-summary. Three types of evidence were considered: example, statistics, testimony. Also, three types of reasons were examined: Motivational, authoritative, expected relations. At times it is appropriate to omit one or more steps if the receiver will probably realize what is left out. This is effective because of the self-persuasion which occurs from active participation in a message. The four-step procedure for presenting a single argument also is used when presenting a position. A position involves a set of related arguments. Three positions for supporting a proposition were explained: Problem-Solution, Comparative-Advantages, Ideal Solution. Three positions also were presented for opposing a proposition: Denial, Repairs, Counterplan. Rebuttal is concerned with defense of one's position. A four-step procedure was offered for rebuilding an argument: summarize original argument, review refutation, present objections, summarize defense.

Exercises

1. Compose a letter to the editor which presents your position on a controversial topic. Develop at least two arguments which follow the four-step format for presenting an argument. If you are particularly pleased with your product, you may want to send it to the editor.

2. Attend a court trial to observe how positions are presented in a court of law. Write a 500-word report on the methods employed.

3. Analyze an editorial in a newspaper or magazine to determine how the position was presented. Was it an affirmative or a negative position? Which type of negative or affirmative position was used? What claims were advanced to support the position? What evidence was presented as grounds for the claims? Were the reasons motivational, authoritative, or expected relationships? Were all of the reasons stated explicitly? Was the editorial convincing? Why?

4. Analyze a print media ad in terms of claim-evidence-reasons. Select an ad that is all visual (uses no words). In your own words, then, state the claim, evidence, and reasons which the visual stimuli seem to imply. How persuasive is this verbal version of the ad? Did the ad "lose something" in the translation from the visual only? What?

5. In about 150 words write an argument on a controversial topic. Use the four-step format. Give the argument, along with a blank sheet of paper, to another person and ask the person to write a refutation to your argument. Write a rebuttal to the attack on a third sheet of paper. Use the four-step format for rebuilding an argument.

6. Keep a log of your arguments for the next week. Enter each proposition argued along with each claim that you advanced for your position on the proposition. What was your evidence for each claim? What were your reasons? Rate the quality of each argument on a 10-point scale where 10 is the highest quality. Prepare a 5-minute speech or a 500-word essay which analyzes your arguments for the week. Advance some conclusions as to how you could improve the quality of your arguments. Be prepared to answer questions from your audience and to take suggestions on improvement.

6

Attacking Other Positions

Refutation is an exciting part of arguing. It involves attacking an argument with the intention of defeating the argument by having it viewed as invalid, distorted, weak, and not serving the search for truth. This activity is at the core of argumentation and without it there is no argument. Refutation is exciting because it is an aggressive form of communication. Aggression commands attention and the inherent conflict in a refutational situation seldom is ignored by observers.

We will focus on this part of argumentative competence by first examining the steps involved in refuting an argument. Next, we will study the strategies which may be used in attacking your opponent's evidence and reasoning.

Attacking an Argument

A four-step procedure will be used for refuting an argument. As with the procedures presented earlier for presenting and defending arguments, this procedure for attacking an argument is flexible. According to what is needed in the given situation, you can omit or modify steps.

1. Summarize the argument to be refuted.
2. Give an overview of your objections.

3. Attack the evidence and/or reasoning.

4. Summarize your refutation and explain how the refutation weakens your opponent's position.

For the first step, give a brief but accurate review of what your opponent said. This enables your adversary and observers to understand clearly what you are going to do. In attempting to refute an argument in favor of legalized marijuana, an example of the first step could be: "You said penalties for smoking marijuana should be removed because medical evidence has not suggested that marijuana produces any more harm than other legal and socially acceptable acts such as cigarette smoking and drinking alcoholic beverages."

The purpose of the second step is to give an overview of your refutation. This is a preview which serves to increase understanding of your attack. For the marijuana example, the overview might be: "I have a couple of objections to that argument. I think the medical evidence that you refer to is outdated. Secondly, I don't agree with your reasoning that we should legalize marijuana because other harmful substances are currently legal."

The third step in refuting an argument is especially important because this is where the actual refutation takes place. Basically, you try to refute your opponent's evidence and reasoning. That is, you attack a claim to show that the evidence and/or reasons on which it is based are not valid. Thus, if the basis for the claim is invalid, the claim must also be invalid. In the second step for the example above, you can see that the first objection concerns evidence and the other has to do with reasoning. There are many ways of attacking evidence and reasoning. We will not try to cover all of them. In the next sections, we will study six particularly useful strategies for attacking evidence and six strategies for attacking reasoning.

Here is how the third step could be executed for the legalized marijuana argument. The strategies employed will be clear once you study the next section. "Let's take a look at my two objections. I think I'm familiar with the medical evidence you cited. It's from a President's Commission for Studying Marijuana back in the 1960's. That evidence is badly out of date. Recent research indicates some serious psychological problems such as inability to concentrate, loss of motivation, and affected reasoning ability. Also, there is the possibility of chromosome damage. Your reasoning about legalizing marijuana because it is not more harmful than cigarettes or alcoholic drinks is not valid. You are saying 'two wrongs make a right.' I am not going to defend cigarettes and alcohol. Cigarettes especially should not be legal. Just because we have some things legal that are bad does not mean we have to legalize other harmful substances. Several wrongs will never make a right. A key point is that you have admitted harm. It seems a bit unusual to advocate harm."

The fourth step utilizes a summary of the refutation to emphasize the damage done and to increase comprehension of the attack. Also, it is important to explain how your refutation weakens your opponent's position and strengthens yours. In our example, this could be done rather briefly: "I think its clear that you do not have recent evidence which supports the view that marijuana should be legalized. Also, you conceded that marijuana is harmful. So, you now have the burden of defending a proposal which will be harmful."

Keep in mind the points made in this refutation. You will recognize them in the next two sections where we will examine a dozen tactics for refuting evidence and reasoning.

Attacking Evidence

We will focus on six ways to attack the evidence in an argument. Although our interest here is in refutation, remember that these methods of attacking evidence can be helpful when presenting and defending an argument since they specify what *not* to do, the mistakes to avoid. It should be emphasized that the following are not the only ways to examine and attack evidence. However, they have proven to be effective and useful methods.

Is the Evidence Recent Enough?

The recency of evidence is important at times while for other arguments the recency of the evidence may not be an issue. If

we are arguing that the President's domestic economic
programs have produced more unemployment than under the
previous administration, the latest unemployment statistics
would be essential. However, if we contend that a past
President was particularly successful at controlling
unemployment, the recency of the evidence would not be of
concern. We would want accurate unemployment statistics
from that President's term in office, no matter how old. Pay
attention to the evidence your opponent uses. It is easy to miss
the mistake of out-of-date evidence. You can challenge your
adversary simply by saying, "Don't you have any information
which is more recent than that?" You do not have to have more
recent information yourself in order to raise the recency issue.

Was Enough Evidence Presented?

Of course, the question of how much is enough is a difficult
one to answer since we probably never can say everything that
is relevant to a given point. In accepting a point, we usually
settle for something less than completeness of evidence
pertaining to the point. What determines when we have heard
enough evidence to accept a claim? The clarity of our
conception of the claim as represented by the evidence is the
most salient point in answering that question. That is, when the
evidence provides us with a clear impression of what is being
claimed, we consider the amount sufficient. In fact, the
presentation of additional evidence after we have reached a
clear understanding will make us feel burdened: "I understand
what you are saying; I don't need more information." Thus,
consider whether the clarity of the conception created by the
evidence is sufficient to accept the claim when deciding
whether enough evidence has been presented. For example,
imagine an arguer claims labor unions have harmed our
economy and cites as evidence a recent wage demand which
was so high that the company closed its plant in the U.S. and
reopened in another country where the cost of labor is very
low. We could argue that one instance is not enough evidence.
How widespread is this problem? How many jobs have been
lost this way? Is the economy actually hurt when this happens?
The evidence requested by these questions would be needed in

order to have a clear conception of the claim that labor unions have harmed our economy. This issue of the amount of evidence is a very useful one because people often make claims based on insufficient evidence. Be alert to that fact and you seldom will be without a basis for refutation.

Is the Evidence from a Reliable Source?

An important way to examine evidence is according to its source. If the source is not an expert in the area of the evidence, or not trustworthy, or biased (having a personal interest in the claim), or unknown, then there is reason for questioning whether the evidence should be accepted. When someone presents evidence to support a claim, one of the first things we should ask ourselves is: "Should I believe this evidence; is it true?" Since it has to come from somewhere, it is reasonable to ask whether the source is reliable. If the source is reliable, we tend to feel the evidence is also reliable. Consider the claim that a company secretly dumped toxic waste on our highways by instructing the driver of a tanker truck loaded with chemical waste to drive with the emptying valve open during rainstorms. A former employee is quoted to substantiate the claim. Suppose further that the employee was fired months before the disclosure. In this case, we would argue that the testimony is not reliable since the source was undoubtedly angry at being fired and might be seeking revenge against the company by charging them with a serious offense. Of course, the claim may be true. However, additional evidence would be required to establish that.

Is the Evidence Consistent with Known Facts?

When we hear evidence for the first time, it is difficult to know whether it is accurate. Given the time and motivation, we could conduct research to determine validity. However, such research is rarely conducted when we argue in interpersonal situations. Short of research, then, how can we evaluate evidence in order to argue? We do not necessarily have to have access to a library to determine if evidence is valid. We can examine it for consistency. Suppose a person makes the claim that the Mafia is still the most influential organized crime group. The evidence for this claim is testimony which shows that although the known leaders of all the Mafia crime families in New York City and New Jersey are in prison, lower ranking family members have assumed the leadership and are carrying on business as usual. It could be said that this evidence purporting to show the dominance of the Mafia is not consistent with known facts that other organized crime groups (e.g., those of South or Latin American origin) have gained a large share of the profits from illicit activities that were once the sole domain of the Mafia. Such a rise to prominence could not have occurred unless the Mafia had lost a significant amount of influence as an organized crime group.

Can the Evidence be Interpreted in Other Ways?

Evidence is sometimes given to support a claim but it is not clear just what the evidence means. In other words, the evidence is ambiguous; it has more than one meaning. The arguer says the evidence means one thing, but it could very well mean something else. Be on the lookout for such evidence because you can develop an effective refutation around the idea that the evidence can be interpreted in other ways. For example, imagine a person advances a claim that a particular diet is an excellent way to lose weight. The diet is a low-carbohydrate, high-protein, high-fat diet, (minimal bread, potatoes, pasta; large quantities of steak, pork, poultry, fish, and dairy products). Evidence to support the claim is a study which found a large number of people who followed the diet lost significantly more weight than a non-dieting control group. The refutation of this could be that the diet is a fad diet that is opposed to the best nutritional information which says our diet should be high in complex carbohydrates, moderate in protein, and very low in fats. The weight loss, in the study cited as evidence for the claim, probably came from some dehydration; some of the weight loss was probably muscle! Our body needs carbohydrates to burn fat. Research shows the diet in question throws the body into a state of biochemical imbalance resulting in things like depression, tremors, lack of energy and stomach problems. People with such problems tend to lose weight, a very unhealthy sign. Thus, another interpretation of the evidence is that the people in that study were *not* more healthy as implied.

Is the Evidence Directly Relevant to the Claim?

At times, certain evidence can seem very convincing. However, the point on which it is convincing may not be the claim made by your opponent. For example, a person might contend that the state income tax should be reduced. The evidence to support this claim might be a thorough analysis of state budget showing an enormous amount of waste. You could attack this by asserting that the evidence really is not directly relevant to the question of reducing the state income tax. Instead, the evidence convincingly points to incompetence in the Governor's office. Further, you could contend that if state income tax revenues were spent properly, according to the major needs of the state, there would be no excess, no room for a tax reduction. Another facet to the question of direct relevance of evidence is that arguers sometimes raise issues which unduly complicate the argument. The issues are side issues, certainly not totally irrelevant, but nevertheless not what the argument is about. Be aware, when you argue, of a feeling that "things are getting complicated." This is usually an indication that evidence was introduced that was not directly relevant, that a side issue was introduced. Point that out. Once everyone realizes what happened, the argument can get back on track.

Attacking Reasoning

We shall examine six ways of refuting your opponent's reasoning. As with the previous section, we should emphasize that these are not the only ways of attacking reasoning, but that they are major and very useful ways. Keep in mind also that you can use these tests to guide your presentation of arguments so that you do not make the mistakes specified by the six methods.

Were Any Important Assumptions Unproven?

When an argument is presented, it is typically based on numerous assumptions. We seldom prove everything that we contend. In fact, it probably is unreasonable to demand that someone prove everything. For instance, if a person says: "This is such a hot day and we will be on the job in the sun for several more hours. Let's take a break and have a couple of cold beers." This proposal is based on several assumptions. Should you demand that the severity of the heat be explained, require proof that you will actually be in the sun for several more hours, or question whether a break is necessary? Probably the only assumption that you would question would be the suggestion to consume alcohol while on the job. That is an important assumption requiring adequate justification. Be prepared in an argument to challenge your opponent to prove an assumption; however, do not issue such challenges indiscriminately. This will make you appear unreasonable. Be sensitive to what the other person is assuming. When you believe you cannot grant the assumption, ask the person to explain and justify the assumption.

Were There Inconsistencies in Reasoning?

Ideally, when we present a number of ideas on a topic all of the ideas should be consistent. That is, one should follow directly from the other. The ideas should be compatible; one thing should not contradict another. This type of consistency in thinking is difficult to achieve. If you discover such a mistake in your opponent's reasoning, you have a powerful basis for refutation. Suppose someone argues that the federal bureaucracy is too large and many functions at the national level should be returned to and managed by the states. The person then proposes to form a Bureau of De-Federalization to oversee this task. This would be an example of an inconsistency, a contradition, since creating more bureaucracy does not logically follow from the idea that the bureaucracy is already too large. Some inconsistencies are not so blatant. A common but subtle inconsistency is when a person proclaims the desire to conserve money or resources but then proposes something which will create a new debt. A husband might say to his wife: "We need to cut our expenses. Although I was going to get a new boat this year, I am not going to. Instead, I am just going to get a new motor for our old boat." The response to this inconsistency might be, "If you really wanted to cut expenses, you would get the old motor repaired instead of trading it in for a new one."

Were Arguments about Cause Valid?

Arguments about cause are typically very important in a dispute, especially for the person who is advocating a proposal. The major causal arguments usually are that the status quo is responsible for certain problems and that the proposal will produce good consequences. If you oppose the proposal, you could argue the status quo has not caused problems and that the proposal will lead to bad consequences. Establishing causality is very difficult. Pay very close attention when your opponent presents a causal argument. The likelihood of a mistake being made which will provide you with an opening for refutation is perhaps greater here than for any other type of argument.

One of the most common mistakes is to propose a single cause without ruling out other possible causes. A well-known example is the argument that cigarette smoking causes lung cancer. To establish that smoking causes cancer, one must also be able to show that other possible causes, such as smokers living and working in areas with more air polution, do not explain the higher rates of cancer in smokers. This type of proof is difficult at best without a valid scientific experiment. A smoking experiment with humans would involve assigning nonsmokers randomly to at least two conditions: treatment and control. The treatment condition would have people smoke and the control condition would have them not smoke. The rate of cancer in the two groups would be the variable of interest. Of course, such an experiment would be unethical and reminiscent of Nazi medical "experiments" in concentration camps. We have our greatest confidence in causal arguments when the evidence for the causal claim was derived from a valid experiment. The more distant our evidence is from such controlled observation, the more question there is as to what produced the results. Since most of the propositions we argue are not scientifically based, the establishment of cause with great certainty is relatively rare.

Another common mistake made in arguing cause is that if A is logically relevant to B, and if A occurs before B, arguers will frequently contend that A caused B. For instance, if a large city enacts a very strict handgun control law, and if the murder rate drops for the next twelve months, it might be argued that the gun control legislation produced the effect of less murder. However, another possible cause could be that the economy improved greatly and people were occupied with work, thus eliminating unemployment which had previously provided both the frustration and idle time which might have lead to angry confrontation and murder.

In dealing with cause in the arguments you present, exercise caution. Seldom say unequivocally that one thing caused another. Instead, you are usually more justified saying, "A probably caused B; A possibly could lead to B; A may have produced B." These examples suggest acknowledging that we are seldom certain when it comes to cause. You should be perceived favorably for revealing such a realistic, careful view.

Were Comparisons Based on Things That Are Not Equal?

We are referring here to arguments by analogy. What was good for one case is argued as appropriate for another case. For instance, we might maintain that the state of New York raised the minimum age for purchasing alcoholic beverages to 21 years of age so our own state should follow this lead. The validity of the argument rests in large measure on the comparability of the cases in question. Usually, if you can show differences between the cases that are relevant to the proposition being argued, doubt about the proposal is created. In our example, the refutation could be stated: "Well, New York and our state are not that comparable. New York has a much higher state income tax and thus has more resources to implement and enforce such a policy. Our state has trouble preventing 18 year olds from drinking. Imagine the problems with 20 year olds."

Was Reasoning from Signs Valid?

An argument from signs asserts that the existence of one thing is an indication of something else. It does not state that one thing *caused* another, only that the two things are related. This type of argument is commonly used with reference to the Problem issue in the Inventional System, especially the first sub-issue: "Are there signs of a problem?" It is important to use only signs which reliably occur and not to introduce causality into a sign argument. For example, suppose an arguer says: "I think our friend Fred is suffering from depression. He said he is having trouble sleeping at night. He lacks energy during the day, has trouble concentrating, and is short-tempered and nervous." Let us suppose Fred is a runner who is preparing for a ten-kilometer race. We might respond to the argument: "You could be right, but I think it is more likely that the symptoms you mentioned are indications of over-training. Every one of those things happen when you push yourself too hard and your body's recovery system is not able to repair and restore the body for the next workout."

Were Emotional Appeals Used Instead of Sound Reasoning?

There is nothing inherently wrong with inciting your opponent and observers of an argument to feel emotions such as fear, anger, pity, joy, suspicion, hope, etc. with reference to what you are arguing. In fact, it is difficult to think of a proposition which we argue in interpersonal communication which does not have at least one closely associated emotion. It is not good arguing, however, to use the emotion *in place of* evidence and reason to justify a claim. To support the claim that you should use your automobile's seat belt, a person might say: "I would hate to see the mess your face would be if you went through the windshield. I could imagine the agony you would put your family through if you were to die in an accident you could have walked away from if you had only buckled-up." Although many of us agree with the claim of this argument, we would probably also agree that the speaker made use of some emotionally charged images instead of the more rational evidence and reasoning which is available for this particular claim. If nothing else works, it might be worth a try to use such tactics. However, a general rule would be that emotional appeals should not be substituted for sound reason and evidence. When it is, a good refutation tactic is to reply: "I understand the emotional side of what you are arguing. Now can we talk about the factual basis for what you are advocating?"

Relating Refutation to Position

Remember a given argument is one part of a person's position on the proposition which we are arguing. Therefore, from time to time, relate your refutation to the person's position. For example, if you are arguing against the proposition that your family should buy a new car, and if you refute the argument that there are problems which can only be corrected by buying a new car, you can relate this to the opposition's case (recall the Inventional System): "I think you still have to show that we really have a need for a new car."

If you are favoring the proposition, with the Inventional System as your reference point, show how your refutation also refutes your adversary's opposition. Suppose you are advocating a proposal to enlist private donations to fight hunger in your community. Suppose also that you have answered your opponent's argument that the problem can be solved by community agencies by showing such agencies do not exist and public welfare has not solved the problem. You could then relate the refutation to the adversary's case: "So, the current system can't solve the problem. It would be nice if they could, but they aren't capable. However, I have a plan which will solve the problem." You then should go on to show your proposal will satisfy the need which you established.

Summary

Refutation is an aggressive form of communication which involves attacking the arguments and positions which other people take on controversial issues. A four-step procedure for attacking an argument was presented: summarize the argument, preview objections, attack evidence and/or reasoning, summarize. As with the procedures from the previous chapter, steps can be omitted or modified according to situational needs. Six ways of attacking evidence were explained. These were based on standard criteria for judging the acceptability of evidence: Is the evidence recent enough? Was enough evidence presented? Is the evidence from a reliable source? Is the evidence consistent with known facts? Can the evidence be interpreted in other ways? Is the evidence directly relevant to the claim? Six ways of attacking reasoning also were taught. These were guided by the principles: Were any important assumptions unproven? Were there inconsistencies in reasoning? Were arguments about cause valid? Were comparisons based on things that are not equal? Was reasoning from signs valid? Were emotional appeals used instead of sound reasoning? These are not the only tests of evidence and reasoning; however, they are common and useful methods. When refutation of a given argument is complete, it is sometimes necessary to relate the refutation to the adversary's entire case to demonstrate the implications of the refutation.

Exercises

1. Write an argument which advances a claim on a position for a controversial topic. Have another person do the same on a topic of their choice. Exchange sheets of paper with the arguments. On a blank sheet of paper each person should try to refute the other person's argument. Use the four-step procedure for refuting an argument. Use the six methods for attacking evidence and the six methods for attacking reasoning. Exchange the refutation sheets. On a blank sheet, try to rebuild the argument. Use the four-step rebuttal format and the methods for attacking evidence and reasoning.

2. Select a letter to the editor from the newspaper. Prepare either a short speech or paper which refutes the letter.

Apply as many of the refutational methods covered in this chapter as you can.

3. Keep a log of examples from your daily interactions for the next week of violations of the six tests of evidence and the six tests of reasoning. Prepare a written report on these violations. Which mistakes in evidence were most common? Which errors in reasoning were most frequent?

4. Attend a court trial to observe methods of refutation. How was evidence attacked? How was reasoning refuted? Is refutation in court different from refutation in everyday interaction? How?

5. Select newspaper and magazine ads which illustrate errors in evidence and reasoning. For each error in evidence and reasoning suggest a more valid form. Discuss how your change would improve the ad.

6. Watch a television interview show such as *Crossfire* or *Firing Line* which has a lot of verbal clash. Write a 500-word paper analyzing the show that you watch. Examine the show in terms of how much was genuine argument and how much was verbal aggression? To what extent were there violations of the six tests of evidence and the six tests of reasoning? How well did the participants refute one another's arguments? Use our four-step refutational procedure to comment on refutation. For instance, was there a step that was not performed well and thereby hurt the overall attempt to refute the other's position? If you were called in to serve as an "argumentation consultant," what advice would you give?

7

Managing Interpersonal Relations

Research has found that a major reason why some people do not like arguing is that they believe arguing is destructive to interpersonal relationships (Rancer, Baukus, & Infante, 1985). They assume an argument will result in bad feelings between people which might cause friendships to break up or marriages to end. Thus, arguing is perceived as a form of communication which should be avoided.

Well, if those outcomes were actually produced by arguing, we would have to agree that it should be avoided, banned, shunned, excommunicated, etc. However, those consequences are *not* the necessary result of arguing. As you recall from Chapter 2, relationship deterioration and relationship termination are effects of verbal aggression. If anything should be prohibited, our analysis suggests it should be verbal aggression. People who say they dislike arguing because it damages relationships probably are confusing verbal aggression with arguing. The two can be mistaken. Both involve attack and defend orientations. However, the object of attack and defense differs, and the difference is crucial: a person's position on a controversial issue is the object in the case of arguing while a person's self-concept is the subject in verbal aggression.

Research has shown that happily married couples argue constructively (Gottman, 1979). Arguing might be one type of behavior which people use to *serve* their relationships. A speculation which has grown out of the argumentativeness research is that arguing constructively serves a relationship by keeping it interesting, creating more understanding of one another, and stimulating people to grow together (Rancer, Baukus, & Amato, 1986).

The idea in terms of interest is that arguing constructively can function to replace the feelings of novelty and excitement which typically fade after a period of marriage. Quite simply, people can become bored or lose interest in one another after a while. Arguing may combat that problem. The inherent attack and defend characteristics of argument almost guarantee that interaction will be interesting. We do not often fall asleep during an argument. A variety of brief arguments throughout the day may be a way that happily married couples "keep things interesting." The notion of *brief arguments* should be emphasized because family communication research has indicated that normal family arguments, that is, arguments not associated with a troubled family, tend not to last long (Vuchinich, 1985). Family members present their positions, attack the positions of others once or twice and then purposely move on to another topic of conversation. This greatly minimizes the chance that an argument will heat-up to the boiling point at which time verbal aggression is much more likely. A speculation which seems justified from research on highly argumentative individuals would be that skilled arguers can argue longer before reaching that "boiling point." Once you have mastered the concepts in this book, you should experiment to see what the "right amount" of arguing is for you.

The second idea, that arguing creates more understanding, follows from the research mentioned in Chapter 1 that arguing improves social perspective-taking (Johnson & Johnson, 1979). When couples argue constructively, they gain recognition of what matters to each person, what values are important, what thinking patterns they prefer. Remember, all of those things are revealed in an argument in the form of claims, evidence and reasons (Chapters 5 and 6). Arguing is, therefore, a form of *self-disclosure*, a way to tell another person about ourselves. Research on self-disclosure suggests that as a couple reveals more and more personal information to one another, trust and intimacy grows (Jourard, 1968; 1971; Wheeless & Grotz, 1976; 1977). In other words, self-disclosure is necessary for people to grow close to one another. However, some people find it difficult to sit down and reveal personal things to another person, even a loved one. So, a value of arguing may be that it makes self-disclosure easier because self-disclosure is a "by-product" of an argument.

The third idea, that arguing stimulates people to grow together, also is derived from research discussed in Chapter 1. This research says that arguing stimulates our curiosity about the topics which we argue so we try to learn more about those topics (Johnson & Johnson, 1979). If one person in a marriage grows much more than the other person in knowledge, skills, or interests, there is an increased chance that they will "grow apart." Differential growth rates over several years can result in two very different people, even though they began the relationship as very similar. Arguing may allow a couple to synchronize their growth rates. That is, when two people argue constructively they stimulate one another's curiosity and this eventually results in more learning for both. Thus, they both grow in knowledge. If one person begins pulling ahead of the other in terms of growth, this becomes apparent while arguing. It will show up in the quality of claims, evidence, and reasons. This may signal the other person to "speed up" a bit, to catch up to the person who is ahead.

Testing Ideas Not People

If an argument is constructive, it results in interpersonal satisfaction and a better relationship. In order to have such an argument, you must attack the other person's *position* on the proposition but *not* the person's *self-concept*. To accomplish this rather delicate task, it is necessary to focus on two things when you argue: the proposition being discussed and your adversary's self-concept. It is not enough to learn the methods of argumentation presented in Chapters 3-6. Besides learning to deal with propositions, you need to learn to deal with people during an argument. Arguing, except in settings like courts of law, is an informal social activity. If you only debated computers, you would not have to be concerned with managing interpersonal relations during arguments. However, you probably are studying this book because of an interest in arguing with people.

A productive orientation to have toward your argumentative behavior is to want to test ideas, not people. To enjoy testing ideas means you have a strong desire to see if something is valid or will work, to find solutions for problems, to discover ideas and truth. Arguing is an excellent tool for accomplishing those goals. For example, the executive, legislative, and judicial branches of our government all make extensive use of argumentation in testing ideas.

The second half of this orientation is that you do not want to test people with your argumentative behavior. To test an idea you can try your best to destroy it. If the idea stands, despite your best efforts, it has survived the test and could be declared valid. Now, it is possible to treat people the same way. You could challenge a person mercilessly and drive them to the point of breaking. Perhaps such a test is necessary if you were examining people who wanted to be secret agents for the CIA. However, to argue constructively, attack and destroy behavior should be reserved for positions on propositions, not people. If you try to destroy people with argument, this is an attempt to inflict psychological harm. It is, in fact, an attempt to be verbally aggressive using the principles in Chapters 3-6. Yes, even principles of rational discourse can be used for a bad purpose.

Imagine a person advocating a proposal that is not well thought out. The adversary, using only the principles in this book, could raise challenges which the advocate is not able to answer and could continue the challenges even though the person has become perplexed, confused, and thoroughly dumbfounded. Further, the person could execute step four of the refutational procedure numerous times (summarizing to show how the refutation has weakened the proposal). If there are observers of the argument, the summaries would give particular emphasis to the advocate's ineptitude. The net effect of the total refutation would be that the advocate was humiliated. Clearly, such behavior is verbally aggressive.

When we try to test people instead of ideas, we run the risk of humiliating them.

Strategies for Managing Relations

Use the Principles of Argumentation with Compassion

I will present several techniques in this chapter for managing interpersonal relations during arguments. The first is to have a sense of compassion when you argue, especially when your opponents are less skillful than you. Do not overwhelm people who are not proficient arguers because you can seriously damage their self-concepts, particularly if an audience is present. The methods of argumentation in this book work. You can win arguments by employing them. But you must know when to stop—and that point is *before* you humiliate the opponent.

There is less concern over this matter when you and your opponent are equally proficient arguers. For those of us who love to argue, it is a great pleasure to argue a controversial issue with someone who is argumentatively similar to us. Here we can "pull out the stops" and see how well we can do. That is, we can test ourselves. Research conducted suggests people who are highly argumentative like arguing with other high argumentatives and really prefer not to argue with people who are low in argumentativeness (Rancer & Infante, 1985).

Reaffirm Your Opponent's Sense of Competence

One way to keep an argument from degenerating to self-concept attacks is to compliment your adversary when he or she deserves it. If the person presents a strong argument, you might say something like, "Your point is a good one, but I would like to offer a slightly different view." Or, "It's apparent you really know what you are talking about. I would like you to consider my position, however." This tells opponents that you respect them and lessens the chance they will feel defensive about self. A *reciprocity norm* typically operates for positive feedback such as this. That is, people feel motivated to give you what you gave them. Thus, by reaffirming the other person's sense of competence, you increase the probability that something nice will be said about you. Arguments, and conversations in general, are much more pleasant when there is an atmosphere of congeniality. As contended earlier, since we usually speak with people we like at least mildly, this type of atmosphere is what we should aim for, and the technique of reaffirming competence works well toward that end.

A word of caution is necessary for this technique and also for all of the others in this chapter. The word is "moderation." Do not overdo it. Too much or too little of any communication technique tends to be less effective. So, for these techniques, as with nearly everything else in this book, I am contending that you must keep your sense of judgment active. "Automatic pilot" works well for some forms of communication such as a conversation about a familiar topic. However, arguing is different. Because of its potentially volatile nature, you need to remain "at the controls" when arguing.

Allow Opponents to Finish What They Are Saying

In communication research, interruptions are viewed as behaviors designed to communicate dominance. That is, when we interrupt we are saying, "I want to be dominant in the situation or relationship." Both men and women interrupt, but some research reveals males may interrupt more (for reviews see Eakins & Eakins, 1978; Maccoby & Jacklin, 1974; Pearson, 1985). This has been explained as a manifestation of male dominance in our culture. Men interrupt more because they have been conditioned by culture to believe that they are more dominant than submissive.

Interruptions can unsettle interpersonal relations in an argument because they might lead the person who is interrupted to believe the other person is trying to dominate the discussion. This violates a sense of fairness because of the "contest-like" nature of an argument. That is, each side should have an equal opportunity to present their case; interrupting infringes upon that equal opportunity.

Emphasize Equality

The possibility of defensiveness in communication is greater when inequalities are evident. For example, two people might differ in status, income, education, etc. People do not like to feel they are in an inferior position. When this happens, they are more likely to be defensive or to interpret a remark or a nonverbal expression incorrectly as a personal attack. Feeling inferior tends to bring out paranoid tendencies in people, and it is difficult to have a constructive argument when people are concerned about possible hostile motives.

When there are inequalities in an argumentative situation, try to de-emphasize them. Sit or stand on the same level so one person does not look down on another. Looking across rather than down says "we are on the same level." If you are sitting behind a desk, change your seat so that you are sitting next to your opponent. A desk emphasizes differences, at times. If you have a title, ask the person to call you by your first name. These are just a few examples. The basic idea is to remember: when two people argue they should not be distracted by inequalities, real or imagined. Coping with the opponent's claims, evidence, and reasons in an argument is a sufficiently difficult task. To worry about things like status differences can only detract from how well you deal with arguments.

Emphasize Shared Attitudes

One of the most concrete findings in the behavioral sciences is that "similarity breeds interpersonal attraction," especially attitudinal similarity (Infante, 1978; Infante & Gorden, 1981; McCroskey, Richmond & Daly, 1975). We tend to like people most who are most like us in terms of attitudes. True, we and our friends are not "carbon copies." However, the research indicates there are many more similarities than differences when two people like one another. One of the best explanations for this, I believe, is that we are motivated to reduce *uncertainty* in our interpersonal relationships. We like to know what to expect from a person. We favor people who have attitudes similar to ours because we know better what to expect from them than from people less similar to us (Berger & Calabrese, 1975). The reason for this certainty is that they are like us, and we know no one better than ourselves. We can more readily assume that if we would respond a certain way to a particular message, so would they. Thus, we feel less uncertainty when presenting the message.

From time to time during an argument, point out attitude similarities. What you are doing, in essence, is telling the other person there is a basis for the two of you to like one another. You can point out similar attitudes very easily while arguing. You can use statements like, "I admire that just as much as you do, but we disagree on...." Or, "I am appalled by that too, but I would correct it in this way...." This tends to reinforce and maintain favorable interpersonal relations and lessens the chance that the climate will spoil to the point where verbal aggression can thrive.

Show Opponents You are Interested in Their Views

One of the dangers in arguing is that we can get so involved in our position that we have little interest in other positions. Because of this we may even become intolerant and impatient with contrary views. This type of stance tends to disrupt interpersonal relations. You feel uncomfortable if you believe your opponent in an argument has no interest in your position and you wonder what the person thinks about other things which matter to you. ("Will this person care if I reveal a problem I am having?") This type of doubt damages interpersonal relationships.

There are several ways you can have your adversaries realize you are interested in their opinions. Perhaps the most important is to look interested while you listen. Do you know what you look like when you listen? If not, you should find out because you could be sending the wrong messages to people by your listening behavior. Imagine a recent argument and look into a mirror to get an idea of what you look like when you listen. Next, practice looking interested. Yes, some of us need to practice looking interested because we may not know how. Look directly at the person; maintain fairly constant eye contact. Eyes should be slightly wide (drooping eyelids can signal disinterest). Nod your head from time to time and use vocalizers such as "um huh." Another way to communicate interest is, simply, to tell the person you are interested in their views. For example, "I'm glad we have the chance to discuss this; I've wanted to know how you would approach this." One of the best ways to show another person you are interested in what they are saying and that you are listening carefully is to *paraphrase* their arguments. (Recall, a summary of your opponent's argument is step one of the refutational procedure and step two of the rebuttal format.) This demonstrates to your opponent that you listened carefully, and such listening is an indication of interest. Interpersonal relations in an argument are less likely to be disrupted if the parties sincerely care about the views of one another.

Use a Somewhat Subdued, Calm Delivery

An argument can be a very stimulating and exciting event. If we allow our voice to reflect exactly the emotional nature of an argument, yelling and loud, overly emphasized sounds might prevail. I am not saying argument should never be extremely animated, boisterous, and colorful. At times, such expressiveness is appropriate and adds to the enjoyment. This seems to be the case when alcohol is consumed as it has a strong facilitating effect in raising the volume level of an argument. However, when arguments get louder, the chance increases that the heightened emotions will culminate in verbal aggression. A reason for this may be that it is difficult to execute the principles of rational discourse presented in Chapters 3-6 if one is highly agitated and emotional.

A subdued, calm delivery is less inflammatory in terms of emotions and more conducive to expressing arguments according to the principles of constructive argumentation. This pertains to gestures also. Non-verbal behaviors should reflect a firmness, determination, but not a sense of emotional turbulence.

Control of Pace of the Argument

This concept coordinates with the previous point about a calm delivery. An argument can get too agitated if it moves along too quickly. That is, the principles in this book teach that an argument should cover certain points (Problem, Blame,

Solutions, Consequences) in an orderly fashion. To go right to
Blame without establishing just what is wrong could cause
agitation because someone or something might be blamed
unfairly. Do not let an argument jump all around the
conceptual arena. A good argument should proceed at a
deliberate and orderly pace through the major issues.

It should be stressed that this does not mean that we should
"drag out" arguments. A deliberate and orderly pace does not
mean the argument should go on "forever." As explained
earlier in this chapter, if possible, avoid long arguments. The
chance of an argument becoming destructive increases with
length. Have an argument move along through the issues. Be
prepared to change the subject of discussion when you feel the
argument has gone far enough. Often, this will mean that it is
not clear which side prevailed. However, the principles of
constructive argument do not say that someone must win the
argument. What is important is that all sides utilize rational
discourse. My research program has not gotten into this yet,
but I believe most arguments in interpersonal communication
should end without a clear sense of "victor." This allows for
the activity of arguing and all of its benefits discussed in
Chapter 1, but avoids dangers of self-concept damage detailed
in Chapter 2. Thus, try arguing often but change the subject
once all views have been expressed on the issues and before
the battle has gone to "the bitter end."

Allow Your Opponent to Save Face

A face-threatening situation is one where we are in danger
of being perceived less favorably. We feel less competent and
perhaps foolish because to "lose face" means we do not feel
justified in having a favorable self-concept. Saving face, then,
means being able to preserve our image when a loss is possible.
That is, we could have "looked bad," but we did not. This
notion is relevant to the idea of "changing the subject before
the bitter end." The "bitter end" means forcing a competitive
situation to a resolution so that a victor must emerge,
regardless of how damaged. Ending an argument before it is
blatantly obvious "who lost" allows the person whose position
did not fare as well to save face.

Face-saving has been posited by social theorists as a major motivation. That is, much of our behavior can be explained as our attempt to maintain or to save face. We should be sensitive to this dynamic in all our interaction with people but especially when arguing because of all the forms of communication, the potential for losing face may be greatest when arguing. Hence, I am contending, use the principles taught in this book and try to win arguments. But, be aware of the adversary's face-saving needs. Press hard, yet stop short of humiliating the individual.

Controlling Verbal Aggression

Recall from Chapter 2 that verbal aggression appears in many forms and it can be delivered in a variety of ways. When we consider verbal aggression, we tend to think of messages spoken with an angry, loud, bitter, sarcastic voice. However, verbal aggression can be delivered in a soft-spoken, seemingly polite manner. Or, the message can be sent by a subtle facial expression. Regardless of its form or manner of presentation, a verbally aggressive message is an unpleasant experience, disturbing the recipient for at least a short period of time or, as explained in Chapter 2, possibly for a lifetime. Our self-concept is vulnerable to hurt, even for those people who have the highest self-esteem. It is important, therefore, that we acquire methods for dealing with verbal aggression in arguments. We will examine five techniques. You should try to master all five because no one technique will be effective all the time. A situation where verbal aggression has been introduced is a most difficult one. It takes more than minimal attention to be well prepared and effective.

Leave-Taking

Once verbal aggression has been utilized against you, the most appropriate response may be to leave. If you think the aggression could escalate, or the costs of continuing the discussion outweigh potential gains, or if you simply do not want to expend the effort it would take to deal with the verbal aggression, terminate the argument. If you do, you have at least two options. You can explain why you are ending the argument, or you can end it with no explanation. There are numerous effective explanations such as, "I have no desire to continue in an argument where I am the target for attack." If you do not give an explanation, leave immediately after the verbally aggressive statement. Do not wait until later because your exit will lose its impact. If a verbally aggressive message is spoken to you and you reply only, "Well, I'm going to have to go," then the adversary probably will experience a sense of responsibility for the outcome. Sometimes this will stimulate an apology along with a pledge not to repeat the behavior: "Wait, don't go; I did not mean that and I won't say anything like it again."

At times, we do not attempt to leave once verbal aggression is introduced. The remaining techniques are concerned with how to return an argument to a constructive track when it has been "de-railed" by verbal aggression. Of course, if we try any of these and they do not work, then our first technique, leave-taking, is a particularly inviting option.

Make the Distinction Between an Argument and Verbal Aggression

Sometimes pointing out the difference between argument and verbal aggression will correct the problem. Distinguishing between the two can be effective. Suppose an adversary responds to your argument with, "Oh, come on, you'd have to be stupid to believe that." You might say: "We had been attacking one another's positions on this topic. Now you just shifted the target to me. Did you want to make a change like that?" Occasionally the simple realization that a remark was interpreted as offensive, especially when it is pointed out, can result in a favorable change in behavior. "Educating" the offender can be an effective means of taking the momentum away from verbal aggression and re-directing the discussion. Another reason for the success of this tactic is that by making the distinction you are, in essence, saying to the person, "I'm on to you." Such knowledge tends to have an inhibiting effect on offensive behavior.

Ask the Person to Justify Using Verbal Aggression

Basically, this involves treating the verbally aggressive message as a claim and requesting that the opponent complete the argument by providing the evidence and reasons. Suppose you are arguing against legalized abortions and your opponent says, "You are heartless to say women will have to live with their mistakes." You could respond: "We were arguing whether abortions should be legal. You just shifted the issue to whether I am heartless. All you did is make a claim. I would like to hear the rest of the argument. What is your evidence and what reasons justify the claim in light of the evidence?" Press this challenge, perhaps until the person concedes. This is a fairly easy argument to win even if the other person is a very good arguer. It is very difficult to prove something about a person's character. So, by turning your adversary's verbally aggressive message into a proposition to be argued, you step out of the defensive posture produced by the attack and force the opponent to defend a usually indefensible claim.

Appeal to Rationality

This strategy for getting an argument back on a constructive track involves asking the adversary to see that the verbally aggressive behavior could change the communication situation from rational to irrational. People generally like to think that they are rational beings; irrational behavior would be incongruent with that image. A way to utilize this notion would be: "If we start talking about the things you just mentioned, we are going to move this argument in a totally irrational direction. There is absolutely nothing rational about you and me verbally attacking one another. Let's get back to the rational discussion we were having." This tactic utilizes motivation to save face. The offender may feel that continuing the use of verbal aggression would result in irrational behavior and would result in losing face.

Refuse to Reciprocate the Use of Verbal Aggression

This constitutes a display of character which says, "I will not lower myself to use verbal aggression and I do not think you should either." This tactic is actually a combination of others because it could involve both distinguishing between arguing and verbal aggression and an appeal to rationality. Here is one way it could be expressed: "You seem to want to change the topic to my competence. I think we would have a destructive discussion if we begin personal attacks on one another. So, I refuse to participate. I am not going to attack you personally in any way."

Responding to verbal aggression is an especially delicate task. The tactics presented here were intended to provide you with some guidance. The research on verbal aggression, although considerable, has not provided us with much in the way of methods for control. Although the techniques presented here are pretty solid in terms of workability and usefulness, feel free to add your own techniques to this list. In fighting verbal aggression, it is difficult to have "too much" help.

Summary

When arguing it is not enough to know the principles of argumentation. Since we argue with people, there is the possibility of damage to relationships. Therefore, it is necessary to know how to manage interpersonal relations during arguments. This is particularly necessary in marriages where destructive arguments can have serious consequences. Constructive arguments, on the other hand, may serve a relationship by keeping it interesting, creating more understanding of one another, and stimulating people to grow together. Constructive argument is based on the orientation of wanting to test ideas, not people. Nine strategies for managing interpersonal relations were explained: use the principles of argumentation with compassion; reaffirm your opponent's sense of competence; allow opponents to finish what they are saying; emphasize equality; emphasize shared attitudes; show opponents you are interested in their views; use a somewhat subdued, calm delivery; control the pace of an argument; allow your opponent to save face. When verbal aggression does occur in an argument it is necessary to have methods of control. Five methods were presented: physically depart from the argument, make the distinction between argument and verbal aggression; ask the person to justify using verbal aggression; appeal to rationality; refuse to reciprocate the use of verbal aggression. Overall, the strategies aim at giving the victim of verbal aggression control of the situation. That is, the "victim" exchanges a defensive posture for an offensive one.

Exercises

1. Interview several couples, married or unmarried, to learn of their views on arguing and the extent of argumentative and verbally aggressive behavior in their relationship. Write a 500-word paper or prepare a four-minute speech which analyzes your interview data. After describing your subjects' views on arguing and their communication practices, draw some conclusions about the constructive or destructive nature of the views and practices. What advice on interpersonal argumentation would you give to these couples?

2. If you are enrolled in a class, groups of 3-5 persons should brainstorm the question: In what ways can arguing be used to enhance a marriage? Prepare a report of your ideas and present it to the entire class for discussion. If you are not enrolled in a class, compose a list of ideas on the question. Discuss your ideas with a friend. (The material could consume conversation for an evening.)

3. Keep a log of your argumentative behavior for a week in terms of the "testing ideas not people" notion explained in this chapter. Record each idea which you tested. Record when you tried to test people. What are the patterns in each category? Are there patterns which you would like to change? When you try to test people, what do you do, what do you try to test, to prove? When people try to test you, what do they do?

4. Write a 500-word paper or prepare a four-minute speech which extends and develops further the techniques presented for managing interpersonal relations during argu-

ments. That is, what are some other ways of managing interpersonal relations? Can you think of some refinements for
the techniques presented in the chapter?

5. Write a 500-word paper or prepare a four-minute speech
   which extends and develops further the techniques presented for controlling verbal aggression. You could present
   methods not included in the chapter or add refinements to
   those presented.

PART III

ARGUMENTATIVE REFINEMENTS

8

Analyzing Your Adversary

A distinction can be made between *expressive* and *adaptive* communicative behavior. When we are expressive, our main motivation is to use verbal and nonverbal symbols to reveal a feeling, attitude, belief, or idea. There is not real concern for an audience as the message is for us, not for people who may observe our expressive behavior. We sometimes do not even care if we have an audience because our purposes are served by both sending and receiving the message. We use expressive communicative behavior to deal with anger and frustration. Such "blowing-off steam" can serve to release tension and improve how we feel. We also use expression when we are confused, disoriented, or troubled. By talking about a problem, we can gain insights into a solution which we sometimes do not obtain just by thinking. Thus, we seem to learn by hearing ourselves talk. Another reason for expression is to reveal our position on an issue because we feel we must say exactly what we believe, and we do not care if we offend anyone by saying exactly what is on our mind.

Adaptive communicative behavior is different. Here, the individual composes messages with a certain person or persons in mind. The message is adapted to the intended receiver. How the person perceives the receiver and how the receiver is expected to react to the message influence message composition. Suppose you say to a friend: "The health club down the street has a two for one special. If we both join, it will

101

cost us each half the regular rate. What do you think?" The reasons behind the suggestion might be that both you and your friend are interested in physical fitness and that neither could afford the regular rates charged by health clubs. Considering these facts probably influenced you in formulating your message. Thus, such a message is adaptive communicative behavior. While expressive communication is only concerned with affecting self, adaptive communication also attempts to have an impact on at least one other person.

The process of adapting messages to people involves audience analysis. This is a major difference between expressive and adaptive communication. Our interest in this chapter is with analyzing our adversary in an argument and any observers of the argument so that we are better able to influence them. It does not seem possible to have expressive arguing. In order to argue, one has to defend a position on an issue while attacking an opponent's position. To attack an opponent's position we have to give at least minimal attention to the opponent and to his or her message. This attention is also necessary for defense of a position. Thus, audience analysis would seem to be an inherent part of the argumentative process. This chapter will not teach you to do something which you have never done before. You have recognized since you were a small child that you need to adapt your messages to the *cognitive behaviors* (ways of thinking) of your receiver. Although you have probably discovered a number of principles which guide how you adapt your messages to other people, some new insights might be gained by considering different perspectives on audience analysis, especially with regard to arguing.

The basic approach of this chapter is to determine cognitive behaviors of your adversary which provide direction for "what to say and how to say it." Cognitive behavior concerns how our minds operate. Undoubtedly, no two minds work in precisely the same way. However, there seems to be uniformity in the ways in which we organize and change beliefs and attitudes and a correlation between changes in specific parts of the cognitive system and changes in other parts.

Before discussing some of the cognitive behaviors which help us understand our adversary better and thus help us in adapting arguments to the adversary, it is necessary to establish a framework for discussing the cognitive behaviors. We will do this by explaining a model of the cognitive system developed several years ago (Infante, 1977). This will provide us with some ideas about analyzing our adversary which will suggest several argumentative strategies. Cognitive behaviors, which operate within the cognitive system, will then be discussed for further ideas about adaptations and additional argumentative strategies.

The Structure of Our Cognitive System

The basic pattern of an individual's cognitive system may be viewed as a hierarchical arrangement with the less important, less organized parts at the lowest level and the more important, more organized parts at the highest level of the cognitive system (Infante, 1977).

Our cognitive system contains many *attitudes*. Attitude is the degree of favorableness that you feel toward an *attitude object*. An Attitude object is anything about which we have evaluative feelings such as good or bad, right or wrong, valuable or worthless, beautiful or ugly, desirable or undesirable. Again, attitude reflects how favorably we evaluate attitude objects. Attitude objects include people, particular behaviors of people, events, organizations, ideas, inanimate objects, animals, geographic places, policies, laws, proposals, and even extrasensory objects such as God, heaven, etc.

The propositions which we argue usually are about at least one attitude object, e.g., Resolved: That a program of compulsory national service should be instituted for all 18 year olds. If you are for the proposition, you want attitudes to be favorable toward the attitude object compulsory national service. If you are against the proposition, you want attitudes to be negative. By understanding attitudes better, we can recognize more clearly why an attitude is changed by an argument or why it is not.

We develop an attitude toward an object when we form

beliefs about the object. Beliefs are perceptions, which vary in strength, of how the object relates to other things such as attributes, traits, characteristics, or abilities. Proposals are usually considered in terms of their consequences. We will be concerned mainly with proposals since, in Part II of this book, we maintained that arguments are about proposals. Beliefs have three dimensions: (1) the *desirability* of the consequence, (2) the *importance* of the consequence to us and to people that we value, and (3) the perceived *likelihood* that the consequence will be produced by the proposal.

Imagine that a person associates the following five consequences with the compulsory national service proposal mentioned earlier: (1) 18 year olds contribute to society, (2) less unemployment among 18 year olds, (3) greater national security, (4) some dissatisfaction over forced service, (5) less freedom of choice. Suppose the person feels the first three are extremely desirable and the last two slightly undesirable. The first three are perceived as moderately to extremely important to self and valued others while the last two are seen as slightly unimportant to self or valued others. The first four are perceived as moderately likely to occur if the proposal is adopted and the fifth is believed to be slightly unlikely.

Given these perceptions of the consequences of the proposal, what is the person's attitude? How favorably would the person evaluate the proposal? Research suggests your attitude will be consistent with perceptions of the consequences you believe are most closely associated with the proposal (Infante, 1971b; 1972a; 1973; 1975a). In this case, the person believes three very desirable and important consequences are moderately likely (this represents a fairly substantial amount of favorable evaluation of the proposal), one consequence is slightly undesirable, unimportant and moderately likely (this consti- tutes some negative feeling toward the proposal, but not a great deal), and one consequence is slightly undesirable, unimportant, and unlikely (this represents very little if any negative feeling).

Considering all of this information, the prediction would be that the person has a moderately favorable attitude toward compulsory national service. My research suggests that our prediction would be reasonably accurate. The idea is that our cognitive system organizes an attitude so that it is consistent with beliefs about the things associated with the object. We did not predict an *extremely* favorable attitude because the three desirable consequences were perceived only as moderately (not extremely) likely and because the fourth consequence was a source of some negative feeling. The fifth did not contribute significantly one way or the other.

How can you use this conception of attitude to guide your argumentative behavior? If you wanted to change the person's attitude from moderately favorable to at least somewhat unfavorable, you could question the individual to determine the consequences associated with the proposal and the desirability, importance, and likelihood of each. Then you could argue claims that the three desirable consequences will not be produced by the proposal (are very unlikely) and that the last two consequences are extremely undesirable and important and are very likely to occur if the proposal is adopted. So, by questioning your adversaries you can discover their beliefs. Once you know their beliefs, you can formulate your claims and attack your adversary's beliefs. This is a fundamental strategy for adaptive communication in argumentative communication.

Values are the final elements which we shall consider in one's cognitive system. A value can be thought of as a *superordinate term* which we invent to give meaning to a group of attitudes. We perceive some of our attitudes are related; they "go together" and represent a group or cluster. A superordinate term is a name for the cluster that captures the essence of what is in the cluster. For example, imagine a person has an extremely favorable attitude toward: regular exercise involving running, swimming, and weight lifting; all natural foods; a low-fat diet; a comprehensive program of vitamin and mineral supplements; outdoor recreational activities. Further, he or she has very unfavorable attitudes toward: smoking; excessive drinking; overeating; pollution of any kind; food additives. It seems clear that these attitudes are related, they seem to go together. The higher meaning of this cluster might be that "physical fitness" is very important to the person. Physical fitness is a superordinate for it organizes and gives meaning to a group of specific objects. Such a superordinate term may be considered a value.

It is important when arguing to determine your adversary's values. These often provide a good source of reasons for our claims (step 3 of the format for presenting an argument) or as a basis for refuting your opponent's argument (step 3 of the refutational procedure). For instance, if you were arguing for a compulsory national service proposal for 18 year olds and your opponent had a strong value for physical fitness, you could base one of your arguments on the notion that 18 year olds will become more physically fit by participating in a program of national service like improving neighborhoods, parks, streets, etc. This would appeal to someone who values physical fitness. In terms of refutation, if your opponent says we should not adopt a national service program because it will reduce freedom of choice (an important value for this person), you could argue if 18 year olds are motivated by the program to become more physically fit they will have more freedom of choice in life, the freedom provided by fitness which will prepare them for a wider range of jobs or activities to enjoy.

At the beginning of this section we said that the basic pattern of organization in our cognitive system is a hierarchical arrangement with the less important, less organized components at the lowest level of the hierarchy and the most important, most organized components at the highest level. Since we have described the components of a cognitive system (beliefs, attitudes, and values) and their specific organizational patterns, we can now specify the overall organization of our cognitive system.

The highest level in the cognitive system hierarchy consists of one or more groups of attitudes. Each cluster of attitudes represents a value that is perceived as extremely important. Each of the attitudes contains very strong beliefs (perceptions of extreme desirability, importance, and likelihood). The next level of the cognitive system contains groups of attitudes which represent values that are believed to be important, but not as important as the values at the first level. Most of the beliefs at this level are not as extreme as the beliefs at the first level. The principle holds throughout the remainder of the hierarchy: the higher the group of attitudes, the more important the value and the more extreme the beliefs. The lowest level of the cognitive system contains all of the attitudes that the individual does not see as related. Thus, they do not pertain to values. These attitude objects are perceived as low in importance, and attitudes toward these objects are easily changed in an argument since they are relatively isolated and not anchored firmly to the rest of the cognitive system.

This model of our cognitive system can be used to analyze your adversary in an argument so that your arguments will be better adapted to the person. This can be used perhaps most effectively with people we know rather well, people with whom we argue frequently. We have more information on likes and dislikes (attitudes), how attitudes cluster, the probable meaning of the clusters (values), and the rank order of the clusters in terms of importance (value hierarchy) if we are familiar with a person. Recall that there are at least two very effective strategies which employ your adversary's attitudes and values: (1) use them as reasons for your claims ("My proposal will result in lower taxes, something you have been pushing for years."); (2) show inconsistencies between them and your adversary's claims ("I don't see how you can oppose U.S. trade sanctions for South Africa until they grant full rights to the blacks there. You have emphasized equality for all people for as long as I have known you.").

This model of our cognitive system has yielded several applications to argument. By identifying some of the cognitive behaviors which occur within the cognitive system, we should be able to further our understanding of the cognitive dynamics of arguing and to gain some additional tactics which may be used when arguing.

Cognitive Behaviors

Belief Change to Attitude Change

In the previous section, we saw that our beliefs about the consequences of a proposal tend to be consistent with attitude toward the proposal. If something happens, such as an argument, to change some of those beliefs about consequences and/or to add beliefs about additional consequences, then the original attitude will no longer be consistent with how the consequences of the proposal are perceived. This inconsistency between how the individual previously felt about the proposal and how the consequences are *now* perceived is disturbing to the person. The assumption is that people try to maintain consistency in beliefs, attitudes, values, and behavior. When they realize an inconsistency, they make changes in beliefs, attitudes, values, and/or behavior in order to return to a state of consistency because such a state is psychologically comfortable. Thus, if beliefs about the consequences of a proposal change and become inconsistent with the attitude toward the proposal, the person may change the attitude so that it is consistent with the new beliefs.

This suggests a basic strategy in an argument: determine your adversary's beliefs about the consequences of the proposal being argued and then formulate arguments with claims which are designed to change the person's beliefs. This was the strategy used in the example in the previous section where we said, in arguing against the compulsory national service proposal, that we could formulate claims which said the good consequences which our adversary thinks will happen will not occur and the bad consequences will happen. Research conducted by myself and others indicates that the more you change the person's beliefs in that direction, the more the adversary's attitude toward the proposal will change from favorable to unfavorable (e.g., Infante, 1972a).

When arguing beliefs about the consequences of a proposal, you need to decide which belief dimension you will argue. Recall, there are three dimensions to a belief about a consequence associated with a proposal: desirability, importance, and likelihood. Which dimension is easiest to change? My research suggests the likelihood dimension can be changed without great effort while the desirability dimension is very difficult to change. To illustrate this in our national service proposal example, suppose a person who favors the proposal feels the consequence "18 year olds having some dissatisfaction" is extremely undesirable, unimportant, and unlikely. According to the model, there are a number of basic ways that you can argue this consequence. You can try to change the desirability, importance, or likelihood. Or, you can try to change a combination of dimensions. Consider trying to change the desirability. You would have to establish that the dissatisfaction would be a good thing. Can you think of a good argument for this? About the best I could think of was, "This type of dissatisfaction over performing a needed service for society will actually be good for the 18 year old because it will serve to awaken the person's sense of responsibility, an important component of the mature adult."

My research suggests this argument probably would not succeed. Arguing the likelihood would be easier and more effective. The person thinks the proposal will not produce dissatisfaction; you would claim it will. For instance: "This proposal is really a plan to draft everyone. There was great dissatisfaction with the old draft system of the 1960s when only a small portion of eligible persons were drafted. Drafting everyone in an age group will produce a level of dissatisfaction which will dwarf that felt over the old draft system."

Attitude Change to Belief Change

This cognitive behavior is somewhat the reverse of the previous one. Attitude to belief change means that, at times, our attitude toward an object changes, but not because we first changed our beliefs (as in the previous example). This can happen in a variety of ways. The person could have a traumatic experience with the attitude object. For example, getting attacked by a dog could change a favorable attitude towards dogs. An individual may change an attitude so that it aligns with the prevailing attitude in a group of people because the person has a strong need for social approval from the group and a great fear of social disapproval. Similarly, a person may adopt an attitude because it is held by a greatly admired person. Finally, an attitude could change (with no argumentation about beliefs) because the person was induced to behave counter to the original attitude, and the person changes the attitude so that there is consistency between behavior and attitude. For example, a person who is induced by a friend to circulate a petition for a disliked political candidate might begin liking the candidate due to the uncomfortable inconsistency of having behaved in a way which was counter to how one felt.

When attitude changes by any of these four means, the new attitude is then inconsistent with the beliefs about the attitude object (remember, those beliefs were consistent with the original attitude). In order to escape the feeling of inconsistency, the person can change the beliefs so they are consistent with the new attitude. In what ways do the beliefs change? Research shows that the likelihood dimension would probably change (Infante, 1972b). For example, if a person favored a proposal to invest money in an oil drilling operation because three consequences were believed to be desirable, important, and likely, and then the attitude changed suddenly due to severe social disapproval from a valued group, the person probably would then change the beliefs so that the three desirable and important consequences would be viewed as unlikely. This produces consistency between the new unfavorable attitude and the beliefs about the proposal's consequences.

How can you use this cognitive behavior in an argument? Perhaps the most useful application would be in a situation where we want someone to return to an original position. This is not unusual. We argue with someone to get them "to go back to where they were." We want to reverse social influence.

Once we realize a person changed an attitude for any of the four reasons specified above, the basic strategy would be to challenge the person for the evidence and reasons which justify the new claims which the person has adopted due to their consistency with the new attitude. In addition, you would present the evidence and reasons for the old claims. Since attitude to belief change tends not to be very rational, the chances are the person will not have a carefully developed position for this newly adopted attitude. On those grounds, this is a fairly easy argument to win. However, what is difficult is convincing the person that there was not good reason for changing the attitude in the first place. If the change was made because of group pressure, the person may feel that was a perfectly good reason. If that happens, a new proposition has emerged: that individuals should allow group pressure to control their attitudes. Your adversary would be the affirmative and you the negative on the proposition. You could define the status quo as independence and individuality and challenge your opponent to demonstrate why we need any other basis for determining our attitudes. Bad consequences such as lower self-esteem could be argued. This also would be a relatively easy argument to win. However, if the person is deeply afraid of the group, you could win the argument but fail to convince the person to change.

Belief Saliency

The beliefs which we have about a proposal often differ in terms of *saliency* and this has some interesting implications for our argumentative behavior. Let us consider belief saliency as the ease with which we become aware of a particular belief. Suppose a person has twelve beliefs about the proposal, "That teaching should be adopted as a career." If asked, "What do you think about teaching as a career?" the person would mention several things. How many? Research on information processing suggests an individual would think of about five to nine beliefs (Miller, 1956). Since the person has twelve beliefs about teaching as a career and becomes aware of perhaps seven of those beliefs, do the five unexposed beliefs affect the opinion about teaching? Could the beliefs that were not recalled be used by an opponent to change how one felt about the proposal?

Belief saliency is thought to be a function of belief strength. The more we think a consequence is desirable, important, and likely, the more salient the belief. Of these three dimensions of a belief, importance may be the key determinant of salience. Attitude toward a proposal is controlled almost entirely by the most salient or strongest beliefs (Infante, 1975a). Since at a given time it is possible to have up to about nine salient beliefs about a proposal, attitude toward the proposal at that time will be determined by the nature of those nine or so salient beliefs. Two points are important in terms of argumentative strategy. First, if a nonsalient belief is moved up to the salient level of the cognitive system, attitude toward the proposal will be affected. Second, if a belief is influenced, especially in terms of importance, the saliency of the belief will be affected.

Returning to our example, the individual becomes aware of

seven beliefs about teaching as a career, and they are all negative: salaries are low, prestige is not high enough, creativity will be restricted, discipline will be a problem, etc. Since salient beliefs control attitude, the feelings at the time are unfavorable toward teaching as a career. Imagine that the person also has five favorable beliefs about teaching, namely, having the opportunity to help people, exciting intellectual challenges, job security, having summers for personal development, and a comfortable work environment. However, these beliefs are not high in saliency; the perceived likelihood that these good things will happen is not high, and they are not believed to be highly important. According to theory and research on belief salience, all that you would have to do to get this person to feel more favorably about teaching would be to make the person aware of these favorable beliefs; that is, simply mention them. By forcing these beliefs above the person's level of awareness, they will play a role in determining how teaching is evaluated at that time. Since the beliefs about importance and likelihood are not strong, the individual will only feel a bit more favorably toward teaching. The person might respond to your brief argument about good consequences: "OK, I didn't think of those things; however, even if they should turn out to be true, they would not be that important to me. So, that doesn't change my feelings much."

By simply making the other person aware of these beliefs, attitude is influenced a little. However, the effect would be temporary. Once your discussion ends, the beliefs would recede in salience and have virtually no effect on attitude. If you want to have more influence than this, there are two basic argumentative strategies.

The first involves arguing the five beliefs about desirable consequences which are low in salience. You would present evidence and reasons which claim the consequences would be very likely and extremely important if the person adopted the proposal of following teaching as a career. Part of an argument on the "job security" consequence might be: "After a trial period you would be granted tenure. Don't underestimate the value of this. You are literally granted a job for life. This represents academic freedom. And you do not get that in any other profession. Former teachers say you do not realize how great tenure is until you take a job without it." If the person accepts your arguments, the believed importance and likelihood of the good consequences would increase and thus they would become more salient. Remember, the more salient the beliefs, the more they control attitude.

What about the person's beliefs about likely bad consequences; should you try to refute them? My research on proposals suggests that you should give most of your attention to arguing that certain consequences are likely. If people accept your arguments, these new beliefs will conflict with older beliefs about what is likely. People then tend to change those older beliefs so that they are more consistent with the newer beliefs and it is not necessary to say much about this (Infante, 1975b). These changed beliefs are less salient because they are lower in likelihood and importance. Thus, they no longer exert as much control over attitude toward the proposal. The desire for cognitive consistency motivates such belief change. In our example once the person accepted arguments about likely and important good consequences of teaching, the person would then believe the bad consequences would not be as likely or as important. The person might say, "Well, I overplayed the bad side a bit." You could try to refute the bad consequences. But do not do this until you have argued the likely consequences and even then do not make your arguments about low likelihood your major points. My research says arguments about high likelihood are more persuasive (e.g., Infante, 1972b).

The second strategy is to create arguments which add new beliefs to the person's cognitive system that are high in likelihood and importance. Such beliefs will exercise control over the attitude because of their salience. In our example this could mean introducing two new consequences: "I would like you to consider a couple of additional points. Through teaching you can have a direct impact on society because you are transmitting culture to a large number of people. Also, teaching does something for your self-concept that few other professions can; you are doing good and you therefore feel good." If the person accepts arguments that these two consequences would be important and likely, they would become strong new beliefs. Because of their high likelihood and importance, these beliefs would have considerable impact on how the person feels about teaching as a career.

Summary

Adaptive as compared to expressive communication involves audience analysis in order to tailor messages to people. This chapter provided a model of cognitive behavior which was used to determine argumentative strategies based on the psychology of the receiver. The model posits that the basic pattern of the cognitive system is a hierarchical arrangement in terms of the importance of cognitive components. An attitude is a fundamental unit of organization. Each is composed of a system of beliefs. Each belief has three dimensions: desirability, importance, likelihood. A value is a cluster of related attitudes. The organization of the cognitive system is that the most important values are at the highest levels and the lowest level involves attitudes unrelated to values. This conception yielded strategies for employing an adversary's attitudes and values in presenting and refuting arguments. Cognitive behaviors which occur within the cognitive system were discussed and additional argumentative tactics were derived. The cognitive behaviors examined pertained to: belief change to attitude change, attitude change to belief change, belief saliency.

Exercises

1. Keep a log for one week of your communication behavior in terms of expression versus adaptation. For each person with whom you talk, record the percentage of your talk that was expressive and the percentage that was adaptive. Write a 500-word essay or prepare a four-minute speech based on this data. What are the overall patterns of expressiveness and adaptiveness? Are there certain types of people with whom you are expressive? Do you seem to avoid adapting to certain persons? What do you adapt to when you are adaptive? How effective are you when you try to adapt to others?

2. Select a friend, someone you feel you know very well. Take a large sheet of paper and outline the person's cognitive system according to the model presented in the chapter. That is, specify near the top of the sheet the person's most important values and the associated attitudes. (You can omit the beliefs as there probably would not be enough room on the sheet.) What are the person's next most important values and their associated attitudes? Once you have plotted your friend's cognitive system as thoroughly as you can, show your analysis to your friend and discuss it. How accurate were you? What were your major mistakes, major omissions? Can you think of some "potential disasters" which could have happened if you had based an argument on one of those mistakes? Did this exercise teach you anything about audience analysis? What?

3. Select a persuader whom you think is especially skillful in adapting arguments to the particular cognitive system of the individual. Describe what the person does. Explain why it works. Are these ideas workable for all people or can only certain types of people do what this person does?

4. If you are enrolled in a class, groups can be formed for formal debates to be held before the entire class. See Appendix E for various debate formats.

5. If you are enrolled in a class, groups can also be formed for informal arguments. Divide the class into groups of 4 or 5 students each. Pairs of students can argue a proposition (perhaps one formed for the exercise at the end of Chapter 3). The remainder of the group can serve as observers and, at the conclusion of the argument, give an assessment. The entire group should discuss the argument in terms of its strengths and weaknesses.

9

Presentational Factors

The purpose of this final chapter is to acquaint you with communication principles, in five different areas, which can enhance your effectiveness in arguing. The second part of this book presented you with the essentials of argumentation theory. This third portion has been concerned with activities to enhance even further your chances of success while arguing. That is, if you only master the first two parts of this book, you will do very well in arguments. However, a mastery of the third part will result in refinements of your basic skills. Thus, the ideas in the previous chapter on analyzing your adversary allow you to "fine tune" your argumentative behavior to the psychology of your opponent. In this chapter, the refinements will come in terms of various message structure tactics, managing your credibility, vocal presentation of arguments, nonverbal presentation, and language tactics.

Message Structure Tactics

Implicit or Explicit Claims

The research on all of the message structure tactics, including this one, is somewhat mixed. That is, there are no clear-cut generalizations which you can follow in structuring every message. Instead, you need to know the various options and then use your judgment in light of the particular argumentative situation. When should you state your claims explicitly and when should you omit the claim and present only the evidence, allowing the receiver to figure out what you are saying? For instance, if you were arguing that there is a need for prison reform, you could cite problems with the current prison system and then say, "It is clear, then, that our current prison system is failing and something needs to be done." Compared to this explicit conclusion, an indirect one would cite the problems but not state the conclusion. That is, it would be left to the receiver to supply the conclusion.

One circumstance where implicit conclusions would be a good choice would be where your opponent and/or observers of the argument are very hostile toward you and/or your position. Allowing the receiver to draw the conclusion makes you appear not "so pushy." Another situation would be where the receiver is extremely arrogant, rebellious, or perhaps defensive and does not like being told what to do or to believe. With such opponents, you might be better off simply advancing evidence persuasively and allowing them to convince themselves by arriving at conclusions on their own. In a wide range of other situations, it is usually more effective to be explicit in what you are claiming (Tubbs, 1968).

Climactic or Anticlimactic

If you are presenting two arguments to establish, for example, the Problem issue and one of them is particularly strong, where should you place it, first or last? If you place it first, then what follows is anticlimactic. On the other hand, if the strongest argument is placed last, your message builds to a climax (Gulley & Berlo, 1956).

One instance in which you should present your strongest argument first would be when you are arguing with someone for the first time and you are concerned about your credibility. In that case, you could put your "best foot forward" since first impressions matter greatly in credibility perceptions. Another circumstance would be when the receiver's attention, interest, and motivation for the topic of the proposition are low.

Presenting your strongest argument first is a bit like "going for broke." You will have little chance for success unless you are able to increase motivation to listen.

When interest in the topic is high, a climactic order works well. When interest is high, there may be an expectation for the situation to end on "a high note." This may be true also when the opponent is somewhat favorable toward your position. The strongest argument last may be the "final straw" to shift the opponent to your side.

Refutation First or Last

When you want to say something in support of your position and you also want to refute one or more of your adversary's arguments, which should you do first (Thistlethwaite & Kamenetsky, 1955)? This matter is especially important when there are observers of your argument. In that case, you want to persuade them that your position on the proposition is superior to your opponent's position. In this situation, a major factor concerns the *momentum* of the argument. If your opponent has made gains and appears to be overcoming your position, the observers probably expect refutation. If you were to begin by saying something to support your position, this would violate the observers' expectations. They would feel you are avoiding what you should be doing, and this would lessen their receptivity for what you are saying in support of your position. Thus, you should first employ the refutational tactics which you learned in Chapter 6. If you are able to execute this effectively, the momentum of the argument will begin to swing in your direction. The observers will then be ready to hear support for your position.

Placement of Disliked Evidence Sources

Sometimes it is necessary to mention the source of the evidence which is presented to justify a claim (see summary of research on evidence by McCroskey, 1969). For instance, in support of the claim that union contracts in the building industry are harmful, I might quote an article from *Engineering News-Record* which gives examples of union clauses which result in some workers being paid double time for doing

nothing. The net effect is pricing homes beyond the reach of the average family. When the source is perceived by the receiver as credible, there is no real problem. We mention the source, the *Engineering News-Record*, and it lends credence to what we are contending.

When the source of our evidence is not credible in the eyes of our opponent, it is a different situation. If we mention the source and then present the evidence, we will have little chance of the evidence being considered, let alone believed. The reaction of dislike to the source will result in an avoidance reaction to all information associated with the source. At such times, we would have a higher probability of convincing our opponent if we did not mention the source. That is, present the evidence without saying where we got it. However, that is not always possible. Adversaries usually want to know the source of particularly good evidence. If you do not give the source, and your opponent has to ask for it, it seems as if you are hiding something. Such a perception can cause more harm to your position than giving the source in the first place.

In a situation where you need to use evidence from a source regarded by your opponent and/or observers as low in credibility, present the evidence, then mention the source (Greenberg & Miller, 1966). This gives the evidence a chance to have some persuasive impact, and the effect tends not to be cancelled entirely by the avoidance response which is stimulated once the source is articulated. In fact, a very favorable reaction to the evidence can improve how the opponent views the source's credibility. In our current example, suppose the evidence on union excesses was from a former union officer who is distrusted by our opponent. After hearing the evidence and then being told that this person was the source of the evidence our opponent might react: "I'm surprised he was honest enough to give that information. Maybe he is not quite as bad as I thought."

Managing Your Credibitility

Often when we argue, we present evidence to support a claim and we do not have a source to quote for the data. In these cases the reason (almost always unspoken) for the evidence justifying the claim is: "*I* am a credible source." That is, we are to believe the evidence because it is true, according to you. If you are not perceived as credible, your evidence is not accepted. Your credibility, then, is a crucial component of argumentative success. If you are not perceived as credible, it is most difficult to succeed in an argumentative situation.

What is credibility? This question has been one of the most thoroughly investigated in communication research (for a discussion see Bostrom, 1983). It has been one of my lines of research for several years (e.g., Infante & Fisher, 1978). There are several approaches that have been taken to understanding credibility (Cronkhite & Liska, 1976; Delia, 1976; Infante, 1980; Infante, Parker, Clarke & Nathu, 1983). We will examine only the major one—the factor approach—in order to specify several tactics which you can employ to enhance your credibility.

The Factor Approach

According to the factor approach, your credibility is the image that people have of you in terms of at least three factors: *expertise* (the extent to which you seem to know what you are saying, possess valuable knowledge, have intelligence), *trustworthiness* (the degree to which the audience feels "safe" with you, believes you are reliable, feels you have his or her best interests in mind), *dynamism* (the projection of energy, forcefulness, and an appealing personality, the impression that you are an interesting person).

To enhance your perceived expertise, there is no substitute for possessing knowledge. You simply have to know what you are talking about. Aside from that given, there are some things you can do to improve this part of your image. One is to mention when you have unique experience with the evidence you are using to support your claims. This tends to reinforce the idea that your knowledge is valid. Can you think of someone who recently used this tactic? I did at the beginning of this section where I said I have conducted research on credibility for several years. Did this have any effect on your expectations for this part of the chapter? If not, as can happen with any communication strategy, this particular one was evidently not successful this time! Another tactic is to make more of an effort to reveal the reasons for your claims. Such care can improve how people perceive your expertise. Still another tactic is to invite questions. In answering questions, partitioning your answers seems to enhance perceived expertise. This involves dividing an answer into parts: "There are three things we need to consider for your question...."

There probably is no easy way to enhance trustworthiness. If you want to be perceived as trustworthy, you have to be trustworthy. There are, of course, some things you can do to facilitate that image. One thing is look at the person with whom you are arguing; some people have a rule not to trust anyone who does not "look them in the eye." Another is to show an interest in the other person. Ask questions about what matters to them. It is difficult for someone to believe that you have their best interests in mind if you have never inquired to learn about those interests. A tactic mentioned in Chapter 7 is especially relevant here. Show sensitivity to the person's self-concept when you argue. This means, in particular, providing your opponent with a way to save face in face-threatening situations.

To be perceived favorably in terms of dynamism you do not necessarily have to be a loud, highly expressive "bundle of energy." You do, however, have to be seen as interesting. So, if you are soft-spoken, subdued, and very calm in appearance, do not feel you can not have an extremely favorable communication image. There is no one type of personality that has a monopoly on dynamism. Like most communication characteristics, you can be perceived as dynamic if you work at it.

Being perceived as dynamic means being seen as having energy. A key determinant of whether you are viewed as having energy is the *variety* in the way you use your voice. If your voice sounds lively, you will appear to have energy and therefore dynamism. This will be covered in more detail in the next part of the chapter. Variety in bodily movements also is a determinant of the dynamism perception. We will examine this aspect in the fourth part of this chapter. Besides use of voice and body, another factor is attitude. In order to be perceived as interesting you should want to interest people. If you make an effort, you probably can be the type of person with whom people like to associate. For instance, do not talk or argue the same topics endlessly. Strive for variety in topics. Do not always be so predictable in your likes or dislikes. Surprise people sometimes. Variety in preferences, in moderation, usually is appealing. Offer to do things for people. This encourages the perception that you have energy. Of course, if your offer is accepted, not performing the behavior will do little to enhance your credibility!

Vocal Presentation

In Chapter 7, we contended that delivery in an argument should be lively while remaining somewhat restrained and calm. This reinforces the state of mind necessary to execute the principles of constructive argumentation. If we speak in a bombastic, highly agitated manner, it is extremely difficult to follow those principles. Instead, such vocal behavior seems to lower our inhibitions about being verbally aggressive. The key is not to sound loud and highly aggressive but to appear dynamic and convey a sense of energy and interest through vocal variety.

Vocal Variety

Three major vocal variables are rate, volume, and pitch. Rate pertains to how fast or slow our words are said. Volume is how loud or soft our voice is when speaking. Pitch refers to how high or low the tone is in our voice. These three vocal qualities, then, vary along three continua: fast-slow, loud-soft, and high-low. The qualities vary, and you have control over the variability. You can control all three vocal variables at the same time. As you are talking you can, for example, slow the rate of words down greatly, lower your pitch, and soften your voice to a near whisper.

Generally, people do not have enough vocal variety in their voices to keep people interested for a long period of time. While few persons talk in the so-called "monotone," most people vary rate, volume, and pitch only minimally. Thus, they do not seem to have much energy, appear tired, and, importantly, seem uninterested. Although a person might be very interested in a discussion with you, if the individual speaks with little vocal variety, you cannot be sure the person is truly interested. Your perception of the person's dynamism will not be very favorable, and probably the argument will not be particularly memorable.

A good refinement for your argumentative behavior, therefore, is to develop vocal variety. Remember, you have control over the three variables which determine how dynamic your voice will be perceived. Remember also, we are not referring to screaming. We are advocating *expression*, the intelligent manipulation of rate, volume, and pitch.

Practice this by giving attention to the key words in your sentences. Emphasize those words by changing your rate. Quite often, we vocally underline words by slowing our rate dramatically. Change your pitch to give emphasis. The change can be to either a higher or lower pitch than the pitch used on the previous words. Volume also can be changed for emphasis. The change can be either to a louder or softer level, depending upon the desired meaning. In addition to the key words, give attention to the rest of the sentence. Put a little more variety into the non-stressed words. This will make your voice sound more interesting. The perception of you as an interesting person is produced because you are engaging three different parts of your voice. It is more interesting to watch a person juggling three balls than to watch the person simply holding the balls.

Vocal Response Matching

When arguing with another person, a potent tactic for increasing the probability that your opponent will agree with you is vocal and nonverbal response matching. We will cover the nonverbal side of this in the next section. Response matching means behaving like the other person. This does not mean mimicry, which is a form of ridicule and hence is verbally aggressive. Response matching means emphasizing the similarities between you and your opponent. Recall that we said in Chapter 7 that similarity is a major determinant of interpersonal attraction. We like being with people who are similar to us, probably because this reduces uncertainty as to what to expect from the person. Thus, we tend to trust the similar person more readily. Moreover, we tend to be persuaded more easily by someone we trust as compared to someone we do not. There is a sound theoretical basis for expecting response matching to enhance agreement with your claims in an argument.

Vocal response matching means adopting your opponent's pattern for varying rate, volume, and pitch. In other words, if your adversary speaks with a rapid rate, with a lot of pitch variety, and a steady moderate level of volume, you would show some of the same tendencies. Remember, this is not mimicry. It is you saying paralinguistically, "OK, if this is how you want to talk, I can respect that and to show that I approve I am going to do it that way myself."

Research on response matching suggests that it provides a way for people to get "in synch" with one another (Moine, 1982). Carried to the extreme, responses can be matched to the point where the response matcher breathes in and out at the same time as the other person. By the way, the research also shows that extremely successful salespersons used response matching while mediocre salespersons did not. Thus, if you are talking with a salesperson (or anyone else for that matter) and you suspect they are using response matching to increase your trust and gain your agreement, here is what you can do if you want to resist persuasion. Make sudden and complex changes in your behavior to "get out of synch." Continue to do this if the person tries to response match your sudden and complex changes. This "breaks the spell," so to speak, and tells the other person that you do not want them to get back in synch with you.

Nonverbal Presentation

Although the emphasis in arguing always seems to be on the words used, our nonverbal behavior during an argument is also very important. The effectiveness of our arguments can be influenced by our nonverbal communication behavior. We send messages to people with gestures, facial expressions, eye behavior, posture, the use of space, touch, time, and the way we manipulate our voices, to mention just some of the nonverbal channels (see Burgoon & Saine, 1978; Knapp, 1980). Sometimes the message sent in these ways reinforces the words that we use; other times we say one thing verbally and another nonverbally. The nonverbal channels tend to be very effective in sending certain messages especially those that pertain to our attitudes. Thus, "fine tuning" certain nonverbal behaviors could enhance the effectiveness of our arguments. We will discuss several tactics.

Use Gestures and Facial Expression

A characteristic of persons who are not very dynamic is the tendency to have little bodily movement when communicating. Not surprisingly, their voices also lack movement, especially in terms of rate, volume, and pitch variation. Being perceived as dynamic is a very important communication characteristic. Communication research by myself and others suggests dynamism co-varies with how expertise and trustworthiness are perceived (e.g., Infante, 1980). That is, the more you are seen as dynamic, the more you tend to be viewed as expert and trustworthy. Recall, perceived expertise and trustworthiness are two major parts of your credibility. How favorably people respond to you in communication situations is controlled to a significant degree by how credible you are perceived to be.

In order to be perceived as dynamic, therefore, you need to have appropriate vocal and bodily movement. We are not saying a great deal of movement. Excessive "anything" in communication tends to be counter-productive. First, determine how much variety you have in your communicative bodily movements. Through this nonverbal "audit" you should get insights into whether you need more movement and variety. If you decide you need more, you can begin by selecting the most important phrase in every sentence or two when you are speaking and emphasize the words with gestures and/or facial expressions. Seeking the most important words for emphasis will get you started. From there, you will be able to work a little more movement and variety into the rest of each sentence. When you have accomplished this, you will have, in effect, increased your dynamism.

Use Higher Status Nonverbal Behavior

Some people (expecially women, it seems) tend to use more nonverbal behaviors which send a message to receivers saying, "I am lower in status; I view you as superior to me." If you tell people that you have little status, you probably will be treated as if you do. You may not succeed as often as you should and you may not be given all that you really deserve. Not being perceived as having status can have negative influence on your effectiveness as an arguer in particular, and as a communicator in general.

What nonverbal behaviors tell the other person we are lower in status? There are several: nodding your head frequently when the other person talks, smiling excessively, legs close together in an unrelaxed position, arms close to body, and gestures with very restricted movement. A more moderate level of these variables tends to communicate that you have higher status: nodding your head occasionally while the other person talks, smiling only when it is very appropriate to smile, legs in a more relaxed position, arms away from the body in a more relaxed manner, and gestures with moderate movement (not tiny movements, but not sweeping either). Start paying attention to these behaviors when you communicate. Are you sending the "wrong" messages to people? If so, it is fairly easy to change. Just follow the above guidelines.

Direct Shoulder Orientation

The people we argue with like to feel that we respect them and have favorable attitudes toward them. There are several verbal factors, covered in Chapter 7, which communicate this to people. Two ways that we send nonverbal messages of respect and a favorable attitude are by shoulder orientation and eye behavior. We will discuss shoulder orientation in this section and eye behavior in the next.

Shoulder orientation refers to the angle of the shoulders when two people are talking. Direct shoulder orientation is when your shoulder are parallel to the shoulders of the other person. That is, you are directly facing the person. Indirect shoulder orientation involves an angle formed by the shoulders of two people. This happens when one person is "turned away" a bit from the other person. Having direct shoulder orientation seems to communicate respect and more of a favorable attitude than indirect shoulder orientation. Thus, if you angle your shoulders away from the person with whom you are arguing, you may be sending a negative message to the person which could reduce the constructiveness of the argument.

Eye Behavior

There are at least three types of messages that we send with our eye behavior. We communicate *dominance-submissiveness* in our relationship with the other person. We look down with a steady, controlling gaze to tell the other person we want to be the dominant one in the relationship. On the other hand, we can communicate a desire or willingness to be submissive by looking up to the person and then gazing downward and performing a bowing movement with our eyelids.

Interest-disinterest is communicated very clearly with eye behavior. Being "wide-eyed" and steady in our eye contact says we are interested while a "droopy-eyed" look with darting eye movements indicates a low level of interest.

Attitude is a third message sent by eye behavior. A "warm" look composed of direct gaze, relaxed eyelids, and perhaps somewhat dilated pupils constitutes a liking message. A piercing look with a good deal of tension on the eyelids would communicate the opposite intent.

There are expected patterns of eye behavior when there is mutual respect and liking between two people. An expected pattern when you are talking is to look at the listener for awhile, then break eye contact momentarily by looking away, then re-establish eye contact and repeat the pattern. The listener looks more, not necessarily a steady, unbroken stare, but more than the speaker's degree of eye contact. A deviation from these patterns can send a negative message to the other person, especially if other behaviors such as indirect shoulder orientation are present. A listener who thinks the speaker is looking "too much" may perceive an unwanted attempt to be dominated. Thinking the speaker is not looking "enough" may produce the feeling that the speaker does not like talking with the individual.

Nonverbal Response Matching

This is the counterpart of vocal response matching which was discussed earlier in this chapter. The theory, as you recall, is that response matching increases the chance that the other person will adopt your position because of the increased trust and interpersonal attraction produced by uncertainty reduction. Remember, also that this tactic is not mimicry, but an emphasis on the similarities between people.

Nonverbal response matching is, in a sense, a "paraphrasing" of the individual's nonverbal behavior. This is showing the person that you understand him or her, which is also what happens when you verbally paraphrase what a person says. On a nonverbal level in an argument, response matching involves reflecting your opponent's gestures, posture, facial expressions, etc. As with vocal response matching, this should be done with sincerity. If not, it constitutes ridicule which is a form of verbal aggression. Done sincerely, response matching is an expression of the maxim that "imitation is a form of flattery."

Language Tactics

The way we use language when we argue has a substantial impact on how people respond to our arguments. You may have heard the adage, "It's not what you say, but how you say it." Well, such a point is greatly overstated. What you say is of great importance. However, the meaning can be modified by how the idea is expressed in terms of language and delivery. We will examine several language tactics which can influence your success as an arguer.

Definitions

Many of us seem to have a strong faith in "mind-reading." That is, we use a word which has several possible meanings, which can be taken in numerous ways, and we have faith that our opponent will "know" which way we intended the word to be taken. A person might argue that "we should get rid of the 'dead wood' in this department." "Dead wood" can mean any number of things, e.g., a person who is not producing enough, a person who does not look good to outsiders, a person who is not improving, growing. This term should be defined early in the argument so that there is no misunderstanding. Two major ways of defining something are (1) to give a specific example of what you mean, and (2) to use other concepts to define your term. Thus, I might use ideas like motivation, abilities, and grade point average to define "academic achievement."

Do you believe in "mind-reading"? A sign may be if people misunderstand you more than infrequently. This could suggest that you are assuming that people always know what you mean. That is not an appropriate assumption when using words which can have multiple meanings. Become sensitive to this when arguing. Explain what you mean whenever there is ambiguity. An argument is difficult enough without creating unnecessary confusion by failing to define your terms. Also, do not let your opponent get away with this error. This is not being "picky." It is a basic principle of rational discourse: "Say what you mean."

Clarity

A related language tactic is to develop a very clear style in your use of language. Some people are difficult to understand. They just are not clear even when expressing rather simple ideas. Clarity is a real virtue in communication. People appreciate it when you are easy to understand. If you can achieve this quality, you will not be in the majority of communicators. Actually, the proportion of people who express themselves clearly is rather small, I believe.

Achieving clarity is something which you need to work at; try continually to improve. In addition to definitions as discussed above, other factors include *abstractions, jargon, simplicity,* and *economy.* An abstraction refers to how far removed a term is from concreteness. Thus, to say, "I will increase your salary 5%," is more concrete than, "I will reward you." Clarity is greater with a lower degree of abstraction. Jargon represents language given highly specialized meaning within a particular group. For instance, "split end" is football jargon for an offensive line position. If you use jargon, explain what is meant for those who do not understand. If you want to develop clarity, you need to be careful about abusing the use of jargon. Simplicity in language is a key factor in determining clarity. Do not use "big words" to impress people. Express ideas in the least complicated language possible. Of course, at times the least complicated language possible will involve some fairly complex vocabulary. The goal is not to use simple language always but to keep language as simple as possible in light of your communication objectives. Economy refers to the degree of verbosity. The basic idea is *be as brief as possible.* Once you master the principles in this book it might be tempting "to talk, just to hear yourself talk." It is similar to looking in a mirror a lot if you are a body builder. However, verbosity is not an effective communication tactic. It can result in people tiring of you. You increase the probability that people will maintain interest if you practice economy.

Provisionalism

Provisional language is the opposite of absolutist language. The latter claims things are certain, there is no room for doubt, and the greatest confidence is justified: "There is no way my program can fail." Provisional language is more tentative, stating things often in probabilistic terms: "There is a pretty good chance that my program will work."

It is rare that absolutist language is appropriate for the propositions which we argue. Things are seldom that certain. If they were, we would have little need to argue. Provisional language is almost always the more appropriate language to use when we argue. If we are claiming higher taxes is a consequence of our adversary's proposal, we could say, "It's probable taxes will be raised," instead of, "Taxes have to go up."

Absolutist language tends to make people defensive and increases the chance of verbal aggression. This is because one of the messages of such language is, "There is no question that I am right and you are wrong." Such language also says, "There is no room for argument." This is not a constructive message and is an attempt to intimidate the other person. Thus, absolutist language can be verbally aggressive.

Summary

Five areas of communication research were examined to determine communication principles which enhance argumentative effectiveness. These constitute refinements of the basic skills learned from the second part of the book. Message structure tactics dealt with implicit and explicit claims, climactic and anticlimactic arrangements of arguments, placing refutation first or last, and when to cite a disliked source. The discussion of credibility revealed methods for enhancing how the arguer's expertise, trustworthiness and dynamism are perceived. Methods for improving vocal presentation focused on greater expression through varying rate, volume, pitch, and vocal response matching. The tactics for refining nonverbal behavior in arguments included use of gestures and facial expression, avoiding low status nonverbal behavior, direct shoulder orientation, eye behavior, and nonverbal response matching. The language strategies dealt with definitions, the clarity factors of abstractness, jargon, simplicity, and economy, and the use of provisional language.

Exercises

1. Keep a log, over a period of the next week, of how implicit or explicit you are in presenting claims. Record each claim argued and whether you were implicit or explicit. Also, judge how successful you were in each argument. Account for the situation, your adversaries, the topic, etc. Analyze

this data to determine guidelines for being implicit or explicit.

2. Describe in detail a hypothetical politician who has low credibility. Imagine that you have been hired as a "credibility consultant" for this person. Write a 500 word essay or prepare a four minute speech which analyzes the credibility problems of this politician and then suggest ways for the person to enhance his or her credibility.

3. Use either an audio or video tape recorder to practice delivery. If possible, record actual arguments. Or, imagine yourself in particular argumentative situations and argue as you would if you actually were in the situations. Then, listen critically to the recordings. Apply the principles of delivery discussed in this chapter in order to draw conclusions about the ways you use your voice during arguments. Determine how well you "measure up" to the standards presented in this chapter. Are there aspects of delivery which need to be improved? Follow the principles in this chapter to make changes. Then use the tape recorder to measure your progress.

4. Use a video tape recorder to study your nonverbal behavior during an argument. If you do not have access to this, stand or sit before a mirror and pretend you are arguing. Picture a hypothetical situation and argue as you would in such a situation. Study your nonverbal behavior in terms of the principles in this chapter. Determine needed areas of improvement. Make the changes and assess your progress.

5. Analyze the audio recordings in #3 above in terms of language principles presented in this chapter. Do you use enough definitions? Analyze your clarity. To what extent is your language provisional?

6. If you are enrolled in a class, students can be paired randomly to argue. Each pair can select a proposition to argue. After the argument, each person should write a candid assessment of the outcome in terms of who won and why. Each person should read the other's assessment and then, if there is not agreement, another informal argument can be held to settle the issue of winning. A variation is that an observer or observers can be brought in to listen to the

second argument and render a decision. Another variation is that a "tournament" can be structured—winners argue in a second round, etc., in order to reach a final round where the two undefeated arguers face each other.

Epilogue

I contended in this book that *arguing is a basic skill.* As a basic skill it should be taught early in the communication curriculum because it is foundational for many other forms of communication such as public speaking, group discussion, interviewing, bargaining, and negotiation. A good deal of research suggests that the consequences of not acquiring this basic skill may be very serious. I emphasized in Chapter 2 that a failure to argue constructively produces numerous destructive outcomes in interpersonal communication, the most serious of which is interpersonal violence. Verbal aggression plays a prominent role in patterns of communication which have violent endings. An exciting possibility, as yet untested, is that if individuals learn to argue constructively, they will rely upon verbal aggression less in social conflict situations. If there is less verbal aggression in society, there will be less of the destructiveness produced by verbal aggression.

I am currently conducting a study of family violence to begin a test of this idea. The hypothesis is that abusive husbands and abused wives are lower in argumentativeness and higher in verbal aggressiveness when compared to spouses from nonviolent marriages. If the hypothesis is supported, there would be a basis for suggesting that training in argumentation should be tried as a treatment for intrafamily violence. About half of the data are collected and, so far, the results look promising.

There are numerous popular books which deal with becoming more assertive, succeeding by being aggressive, and protecting self from verbal attack. A characteristic which is disturbing in some of this work is that instead of teaching the principles of rational discourse, the authors instruct on techniques of verbal aggression (personal attacks). This book distinguished argument from verbal aggression and emphasized the destructiveness of attacking another person's self-concept. A typical lesson in some books goes something like this: A man pronounces to a woman, "You should not go into engineering; women can't handle the math and science." The woman is told to respond, "I'm shocked to hear an outmoded view like that coming from you; but, then, that's a typical view of older men, so you should not feel strange."

A major problem with such teaching is that the person is told to use verbal aggression in response to verbal aggression; thus, destructiveness is encouraged. Two wrongs do not make a right, and such reciprocity increases the chance of escalating aggression in the interpersonal relationship. This book taught the use of constructive argumentation in resolving controversial issues. Thus, in our example, it would be a mistake to try to make the man feel incompetent for having such a view of engineering and woman. If someone said something like that to you, using the system presented in this book, you could deal constructively with the issue. Briefly, you would ask him, in a nondemanding voice, to be specific in terms of exactly what he is *claiming*. If this clarity is ever achieved, you would request *evidence* which is unequivocal grounds for the claim, and then ask for *reasons* why the evidence warrants the claim. You would apply six tests to the evidence and six tests to the reasoning. This analysis would provide a basis for arguing—for challenging the evidence and reasoning. You would make this *a search for the truth* so when he realizes his position cannot be defended, he will abandon it without the resentment which is produced by verbal aggression. This would be a very easy argument to win. There simply is no excuse here for resorting to a personal attack. As I maintained in this book, verbal aggression is very harmful and is unnecessary now that you know how to argue. You will prevail more completely in social situations by arguing constructively.

Interestingly, when I first began doing research on argumentativeness as a personality trait in the late 1970s I nearly omitted verbal aggressiveness from the model because the distinction between argument and verbal aggression seemed so obvious. Discussions with Dr. Andrew Rancer, then my doctoral student and now a professor at Emerson College, convinced me that what seems so apparent is not to many people and this failure to discriminate the locus of attack is a major reason why there is confusion concerning argument. We were later interviewed on several radio and television talk shows and the idea that seemed to create the most interest was the argumentativeness-verbal aggressiveness distinction. This increased awareness of destructive forms of communication is encouraging because the communication discipline does have the pedagogy to correct such problems. (One example is the material in Chapters 3-6.) The discipline has specialized for more than 2500 years in teaching people how to communicate in a constructive manner.

The most fundamental thing which I have tried to accomplish in this book is to teach a *preference for rational discourse.* In addition to what we have studied, there are many other ways of advocating a position on a controversial issue: using appeals which make use of feelings of prejudice, fear, hate, and hostility; telling people what to believe and not allowing them to join in the search for an answer; threatening those who hold minority views; gaining compliance for a position by physical force such as taking hostages; and, a form we have discussed extensively, trying to damage another position by injuring the self-concept of the person who holds the position.

What is "rational" about the way of communicating taught in this book? There are several characteristics which deserve to be categorized as rational rather than irrational: defining the conflict in order to avoid ambiguity and misunderstanding; emphasizing that claims must be based on evidence, with rigorous tests for the evidence; giving close attention to the reasons for claims, with rigorous standards for reasoning; stressing that the individual's self-concept is not a proper target for attack; maintaining that the tools of argumentation theory are to be used to discover knowledge.

This latter point means the principles taught in this book

represent a *way of knowing.* How do we determine, for example, a plan for eliminating hunger in this country? The answer is, through argumentation. The approach to the problem of hunger which survives debate at the various levels of government is assumed to be the superior solution. This is "survival of the fittest" in terms of ideas. The United States is structured around the idea that freedom of speech provides the communication climate for a wide variety of ideas which can be tested by argumentation to determine which is best. The system works so well that few in this country would have it any other way.

Despite the fact that freedom of speech and the use of argumentation are so successful at the national level, those principles are infrequently followed in organizations, companies, and in families. My colleagues and I have developed an Employee Rights Scale to study employees who are expected to "check their rights as U.S. citizens at the door" when they go to work (Gorden, Infante, Wilson & Clarke, 1984). Generally, we have found that when employees' rights are violated, they tend to have superiors who are verbally aggressive and who dislike genuine argument (Gorden & Infante, 1987). Moreover, employees with violated rights are less satisfied with their jobs, superiors, and careers.

This application of the argumentativeness and verbal aggressiveness models to communication in organizations is currently my major research interest. My colleague, Dr. William Gorden of Kent State University, and I have recently completed several studies (so recent that they are not yet published). Some of the results were very interesting and very supportive of the premise of this book concerning the constructiveness of argumentativeness and the destructiveness of verbal aggressiveness. In one study we asked about 150 superiors in a variety of organizations to rate a subordinate with whom the superior is either satisfied, dissatisfied, or undecided regarding the subordinate's job performance. The results supported the counterintuitive hypothesis that when superiors were dissatisfied with subordinates the subordinates would be lower in argumentativeness when compared to subordinates with whom the superior is satisfied in terms of job performance. The hypothesis is counterintuitive because of the belief that "you should not argue with your boss if you want to succeed." Another counterintuitive hypothesis that was supported in this study was that subordinates having a "complainer" as compared to a "constructive" disagreement style, according to superiors, would be lower in argumentativeness. Thus, liking to argue does not mean that one also is a complainer. The results for verbal aggressiveness were as predicted and emphasize that it does one little good to be verbally aggressive. That is, when subordinates were higher in verbal aggressiveness they were more likely to be judged by their superior as not performing their job satisfactorily and they were more likely to be identified by their superior as being a complainer.

In another study, Gorden and I extended earlier research (Infante & Gorden, 1985a; 1985b) which found superiors who were higher in argumentativeness and lower in verbal aggressiveness were more successful in several ways. We found in the most recent research that higher argumentativeness and lower verbal aggressiveness is especially effective in organizational communication when accompanied by an *affirming communicator style*. Such a style involves being highly relaxed, attentive, and friendly. I was happy to observe these results because they support several speculations which I made in this book (the data were gathered after I completed the nine chapters). That is, arguing is more productive when it is not agitated, is subdued to a degree (relaxed), and we analyze our adversaries, demonstrate that what they say matters (attentive), and we are nice, do not inflict psychological hurt (friendly). I believe this research is revealing because it suggests a style, and not a simplistic one, that seems to attract good outcomes: be argumentative but with an affirming communicator style (low in verbal aggression but highly relaxed, attentive, and friendly).

The principles of argumentation work in the legislative, executive, and judicial branches of all levels of our government. They also work in interpersonal relations, families, companies, and organizations. The research summarized in Chapter 1 suggests that arguing constructively has numerous benefits; no context appears excluded. Thus, you may use the principles of rational discourse which you have learned from this book in all aspects of your life, in interpersonal relationships, in your family, on the job, and as a participant in a democracy.

In order for you actually to acquire this preference for rational discourse I believe you need to find that it works better for you than other ways of communicating. In order to discover that, *you need to use the system taught in this book.* It will only do something for you if you give it a chance. To use the system you need to know it thoroughly.

If you have an adequate grasp of the principles of arguing constructively, you should be able to answer each of the following questions without hesitation and without turning back to earlier parts of this book.

1. What are the five parts of constructive argumentation? (Just name the parts without elaboration, and do not go to the next question until you answer this one.)
2. What is the rationale for stating a controversy in propositional form?
3. In the Inventional System, what are the four major issues? What are the sub-issues of each major issue?
4. What are the three basic positions that you can take if you are affirmative on a proposition?
5. What are the three basic positions that you can take if you are negative on a proposition?
6. What is the format for presenting an argument?
7. What is the format for refuting an argument?
8. What is the format for rebuilding an argument?
9. What are the major ways of attacking evidence?
10. What are the major ways of attacking reasoning?
11. What are the principles of managing interpersonal relations during arguments?
12. What are the essential distinctions between argument and verbal aggression?

When you are able to answer these twelve questions, you have a cognitive grasp of constructive argumentation. However, having cognitive knowledge does not necessarily mean that you are able to argue constructively. In order to acquire the behaviors designated by argumentation theory you must *practice* employing the principles. Practice will result in simulating the thoughts and feelings that you should have during an argument. Connections will be made in your nervous system between your brain activity and motor responses. Thus, you will be able to do what you think you should do. After a period of time you will become attuned to the thoughts and feelings; you will know the thought and feeling sensations of arguing constructively. When this happens, you will not have to think about the mechanics of arguing such as the four-step format for refutation. You will be able to do it naturally.

You are near the end of this book. Have you decided whether to establish the pathways between brain activity and actual motor response? The decision is yours. If you do not wish to use argumentation theory in your life, I believe the knowledge of argumentation which you gained from this book will enhance your understanding of your social universe. Knowledge for the sake of knowledge is a valid reason for studying something. Knowledge does not have to result in some concrete benefit, some observable consequence. Simply understanding something better is an excellent justification for effort expended in study.

On the other hand, if you wish to enhance your argumentative behavior, there is ample reason for doing so. Research summarized in Chapter 1 suggests there are numerous favorable consequences associated with constructive argumentation. If you make the effort to actualize what you have studied in this book, you will soon realize that the principles are powerful; they work. Possessing the tools taught in this book will provide you with feelings of power and confidence because you will believe that you are able to influence your environment. As a result, you probably will not have feelings of helplessness in dealing with your social universe because your skills justify the feeling that you can exercise control. When this happens you will truly feel comfortable with the methods of constructive argumentation; you will have a strong belief that these methods are the best way for dealing with controversy. You will possess a preference for rational discourse.

Glossary

A brief explanation is given for the major terms used in this book. Words in the definitions which are in italics are included as entries in the Glossary.

Absolutist language Claims things are certain to happen, makes *argument* appear unwanted.

Adaptive communication Selection of verbal and nonverbal symbols for messages is influenced by the intended receiver.

Affirmative A *position* which favors what is asserted by a *proposition*.

Allowing opponent to save face A strategy for managing interpersonal relations during arguments by enabling the adversary to preserve a favorable image when a loss is possible.

Analogy An expected relationship where because two things are similar what is true for one is assumed also true for the other.

Analysis The process of examining a *proposition* to determine the possible *positions, issues,* and *arguments.*

Anticlimactic arrangement Strongest *argument* is placed first in a message.

Appeal to rationality A method of controlling *verbal aggression* which utilizes peoples' desire to appear rational.

Arguing Presenting and defending *positions* on controversial issues while attacking the *positions* which other people take on the issues.

Argument   Used two ways: as a message which *claims* something based on *evidence* and reasoning, as interaction between people where they attack one another's *positions* on an issue.

Argumentation   Argument which employs the principles and procedures of *argumentation theory.*

Argumentation theory   A set of principles and procedures of *rational discourse* for conflict situations which have evolved from the time of Ancient Greece.

Argumentative approach   An approach to controversy which involves informative and persuasive efforts in addition to attacking an adversary's *position.*

Argumentativeness   A personality trait which involves presenting and defending *positions* on controversial issues while attacking the positions which other people take on the issues. A subset of *assertiveness.*

Argumentative skill deficiency   A cause of *verbal aggression* where a person employs self-concept attacks on others due to frustration in not being skilled at attacking and defending *positions* on controversial issues.

Ask for justification of verbal aggression   A method of controlling *verbal aggression* by turning the offender's verbally aggressive message into a *proposition* to be argued.

Assertiveness   The personality trait to be interpersonally dominant, ascendant, and forceful.

Attack-and-defend orientation   The basic mental set which people assume when arguing.

Attitude   How favorably an *attitude object* is evaluated. A predisposition to respond in a consistently favorable or unfavorable way toward an attitude object.

Attitude change to belief change   A *cognitive behavior* where *attitude* change leads to changes in the *beliefs* about the *attitude object.*

Attitude object   Anything about which an *attitude* is formed.

Audience analysis   Determining the probable *beliefs, attitudes,* and *values* of an audience so message appeals can be developed which will motivate the audience to accept the communicator's *position.*

Avoid interruptions   A strategy for managing interpersonal relations during *arguments* which creates a sense of equal opportunity and a lack of domination by the participants.

Belief   Represents perceptions of the attributes of an *attitude object.* Beliefs vary in terms of desirability, importance, and likelihood.

Belief change to attitude change   A *cognitive behavior* where *belief* influence leads to *attitude* influence.

Belief saliency   A *cognitive behavior* that pertains to how easily we become aware of a *belief.*

Benefit of presumption The assumption granted to the negative for a *proposition* that the *status quo* is adequate and should not be changed unless proven otherwise.

Brief arguments A characteristic of constructive arguments in normal families.

Burden of proof Obligation of the person who is *affirmative* for the *proposition* to present a logically complete case supporting the proposition.

Cause not valid A way of attacking reasoning which shows that other possible causes for something were not ruled out.

Claim The part of an *argument* which says what is being concluded, what the argument is about in terms of its point.

Classification An expected relationship where what is true for a class is assumed to be true for each member of the class.

Climactic arrangement The strongest *argument* in a message is placed last.

Cognitive behaviors Ways in which the mind operates, ways of thinking.

Cognitive system Structure of *beliefs, attitudes,* and *values* which is in the form of a hierarchy with the most important value and associated attitudes in the highest position.

Communication When people use verbal and nonverbal symbols to stimulate meaning in other people.

Comparative-advantages A *position* for supporting a *proposition* which maintains the *issue* is not that there is a problem but that a proposed policy can result in advantages that are not being produced by the *status quo.*

Comparison of things not equal A way of attacking reasoning which shows the basis for an *analogy* is invalid because the cases are not comparable.

Compassion A strategy for managing interpersonal relations during *arguments* which emphasizes stopping before one's adversary is humiliated.

Compliance-gaining strategies Tactics such as the use of promises, threats, and guilt in conflict situations.

Consistency of evidence A way of attacking *evidence* that assesses whether the information is corroborated by other evidence.

Constructive argument *Argument* which follows the principles and procedures of *rational discourse* and results in good consequences.

Control the pace of an argument A strategy for managing interpersonal relations during *arguments* based on the idea of avoiding agitation.

Counterplan   A *position* for opposing a *proposition* which agrees that there are serious problems and offers an alternative to the *affirmative's* plan for solving the problems.

Credibility   Often conceived as a set of *attitudes* that a receiver has about a source's expertise, trustworthiness, and dynamism.

Critical thinking mind-set   Actively testing objects of judgment by applying criteria such as found in a *system of analysis*.

Denial   A *position* for opposing a *proposition* which maintains there is no need for a proposal and that the proposal would not work even if there was a need.

Disdain   A cause of *verbal aggression* where strong dislike for a person motivates personal attacks.

Emotional appeals   A way of attacking reasoning which maintains emotion was used in place of evidence and reasoning to justify a *claim*.

Emphasize equality   A strategy for managing interpersonal relations during *arguments* which avoids the defensiveness created by status differences.

Emphasize shared attitudes   A strategy for managing interpersonal relations during *arguments* based on the principle that similarity breeds interpersonal attraction.

Evidence   Information used to support a *claim*: example, statistics, testimony.

Explicit claim   *Evidence* is presented along with a clear statement of the *claim*.

Expression   Varying vocal rate, volume, and pitch in order to enhance the meaning of a message.

Expressive communication   Use of verbal and nonverbal symbols to reveal thinking and feelings with no concern for other people getting meaning from the symbols.

Eye behavior   Communicates at least three types of messages: dominance-submission, interest-disinterest, like-dislike.

Fact   A type of *proposition* which proposes that something can be declared either true or false, existent or nonexistent. Can pertain to the past, present, or future.

High argumentatives   People who have strong motivation to approach *arguments* and weak motivation to avoid them.

Hostility   The personality trait to use verbal and nonverbal symbols to express irritability, negativism, resentment, and suspicion.

Ideal solution   A *position* for supporting a *proposition* which specifies criteria for an ideal solution and attempts to demonstrate that the proposed solution best satisfies the criteria.

Implicit claim   *Evidence* is presented and the receiver is left to determine what is being claimed.

Inconsistencies in reasoning A way of attacking reasoning which points out contradictions when one thing does not follow from something it normally is associated with.

Informative approach An approach to controversy which involves stating one's *position* so other people can understand the position. There is no attempt to persuade people regarding the position.

Interpretation of evidence. A way of attacking *evidence* that deals with whether the evidence is ambiguous, has more than one meaning.

Invention The process of discovering *arguments* which originated in Ancient Greece and Rome.

Inventional system A *system of analysis* which utilizes four general *issues:* problem, blame, solution, consequences.

Issue A major area of disagreement for the individuals arguing a *proposition.* Determining the issues in an *argument* is important in order for the argument to be constructive.

Jargon Language given highly specialized meaning within a particular group.

Leave-taking A method of controlling *verbal aggression* when the costs of continuing the discussion outweigh the potential gains.

Locus of attack The place or target of attack. In an *argument* the place of attack is the person's *position* while the person's self-concept is the target in *verbal aggression.*

Low argumentatives People who have weak motivation to approach *arguments* and strong motivation to avoid them.

Making the distinction between argument and verbal aggression A method of controlling *verbal aggression* which educates the offender and allows the victim to regain momentum in the *argument.*

Moderate argumentatives People who have approximately equal approach and avoidance motivation for arguments. Two types: Conflicting Feelings (high on both approach and avoidance); Apathetic (low on both approach and avoidance).

Negative A *position* which opposes what is asserted by a *proposition.*

Nonverbal response matching Behaving nonverbally in a manner which is similar to another person in order to create trust through perceived similarity.

Paralinguistics The ways in which the voice is used in communication.

Persuasive approach An approach to controversy which involves explaining a *position* in order to influence other people to adopt the position.

Policy A type of *proposition* which proposes a course of action.

Positions The *affirmative* or *negative* sides of *propositions* which people defend or attack.

Presenting an argument Four steps are involved: *claim-evidence-reasons-summary.*

Problem-solution A *position* for supporting a *proposition* which entails demonstrating that there is a need for a change and that the *affirmative's* proposal will satisfy the need and thus solve the problem.

Proposal What is made by someone who is *affirmative* on a *proposition* to those who are negative on the proposition.

Proposition A statement of a controversial issue. There are three types: *fact, value,* and *policy.* Each represents a type of proposal.

Provisional language Leaves room to doubt a claim, thus encouraging the possibility of *argument.*

Psychopathology A cause of *verbal aggression* where a target is created to symbolize a source of hurt which was repressed due to an inability at the time to retaliate.

Quantity of evidence A way of attacking *evidence* that pertains to the clarity created for the *claim.*

Rational discourse Communication based on valid *evidence* and reasoning which avoids excessive reactions in receivers and encourages people to search for knowledge and understanding regarding a controversial issue.

Reaffirm opponent's competence A strategy for managing interpersonal relations during *arguments* which entails deserved praise in order to create a congenial and supportive climate for argument.

Reasons Why it is that certain *evidence* can be said to suggest a given claim. There are three types: motivational, authoritative, expected relations.

Rebuttal Rebuilding a position or argument which was the object of refutation. Four steps are involved: summarize original argument, review refutation, present objections, summarize defense.

Recency of evidence A way of attacking *evidence* that calls attention to whether the evidence is out of date.

Refuse to reciprocate verbal aggression A method of controlling *verbal aggression* which emphasizes good character and a desire to maintain rationality.

Refutation The process of attacking an *argument* or *position.* Four steps are involved: summarize the *argument,* preview the objections, attack *evidence* and/or reasoning, summarize.

Relevance of evidence A way of attacking *evidence* which determines whether the evidence applies better to another claim which is actually irrelevant to the proposition.

Reliability of source A way of attacking *evidence* that focuses on the expertise and trustworthiness of the source of information.

Repairs A *position* for opposing a *proposition* which agrees there are some problems but that they can be solved by some relatively minor changes in the *status quo* rather than a radical change proposed by the *affirmative.*

Self-concept damage The most fundamental effect of *verbal aggression.*

Self-disclosure The process in interpersonal communication of revealing self to others. Under conditions of reciprocal support and disclosure, trust and intimacy grows in a relationship.

Showing an interest in opponent's views A strategy for managing interpersonal relations during *arguments* which communicates respect, attentiveness, and goodwill toward the adversary.

Signs and their meaning A way of attacking reasoning which claims the signs of a problem cited are not reliable indicators of the supposed problem.

Social learning A cause of *verbal aggression* where the individual learns verbally aggressive messages through a process of direct and also vicarious reinforcement.

Sources of evidence Four major sources: personal experience, testimony, electronic media, print media.

Status quo The present system or the present state of affairs. The thing which the *proposition* asserts should be modified or changed.

System of analysis A set of general *issues* which are applied to a *proposition* in order to create *arguments.* This is part of the *invention* process.

Testing ideas not people A necessary cognitive orientation in order to have *constructive argument.*

Unproven assumptions A way of attacking reasoning which determines if all assumptions for a case were proven.

Use a calm delivery A strategy for managing interpersonal relations during *arguments* which lessens the chance a verbal fight will result from excessive emotionality.

Value The meaning given to a group of related *attitudes.* Also, a type of *proposition* which proposes something should be viewed favorably or unfavorably.

Verbal aggression A message which attacks the self-concept of the receiver in order to inflict psychological pain and have the individual feel unfavorably about self.

Verbal aggressiveness The personality trait which involves attacking the self-concepts of individuals with verbal and nonverbal messages. A subset of *hostility.*

Vocal response matching Behaving vocally in a manner which is similar to another person's vocal behavior in order to create trust through perceived similarity.

Appendix

Appendix A

Argumentativeness Scale*

Instructions

This questionnaire contains statements about arguing controversial issues. Indicate how often each statement is true for you personally by placing the appropriate number in the blank to the left of the statement. If the statement is *almost never true* for you, place a "1" in the blank. If the statement is *rarely true* for you, place a "2" in the blank. If the statement is *occasionally true* for you, place a "3" in the blank. If the statement is *often true* for you, place "4" in the blank. If the statement is *almost always true* for you, place a "5" in the blank.

_____ 1. While in an argument, I worry that the person I am arguing with will form a negative impression of me.

_____ 2. Arguing over controversial issues improves my intelligence.

_____ 3. I enjoy avoiding arguments.

_____ 4. I am energetic and enthusiastic when I argue.

_____ 5. Once I finish an argument I promise myself that I will not get into another.

---

*From: Infante, D.A., & Rancer, A.S. (1982). A conceptualization and measure of argumentativeness. *Journal of Personality Assessment, 46,* 72-80. Reproduced with permission of the authors.

_____   6. Arguing with a person creates more problems for me than it solves.

_____   7. I have a pleasant, good feeling when I win a point in an argument.

_____   8. When I finish arguing with someone I feel nervous and upset.

_____   9. I enjoy a good argument over a controversial issue.

_____   10. I get an unpleasant feeling when I realize I am about to get into an argument.

_____   11. I enjoy defending my point of view on an issue.

_____   12. I am happy when I keep an argument from happening.

_____   13. I do not like to miss the opportunity to argue a controversial issue.

_____   14. I prefer being with people who rarely disagree with me.

_____   15. I consider an argument an exciting intellectual challenge.

_____   16. I find myself unable to think of effective points during an argument.

_____   17. I feel refreshed and satisfied after an argument on a controversial issue.

_____   18. I have the ability to do well in an argument.

_____   19. I try to avoid getting into arguments.

_____   20. I feel excitement when I expect that a conversation I am in is leading to an argument.

Appendix B

Argumentativeness Scoring

1. Add your scores on items: 2, 4, 7, 9, 11, 13, 15, 17, 18, 20
2. Add 60 to the sum obtained in step 1
3. Add your scores on items: 1, 3, 5, 6, 8, 10, 12, 14, 16, 19
4. To compute your argumentativeness score, subtract the total obtained in step 3 from the total obtained in step 2

Interpretation:

73-100 = High in Argumentativeness
56-72 = Moderate in Argumentativeness
20-55 = Low in Argumentativeness

Appendix							**153**

Appendix C

Verbal Aggressiveness Scale*

This survey is concerned with how we try to get people to comply with our wishes. Indicate how often each statement is true for you personally when you try to influence other persons. Use the following scale:

> 1 - almost never true
> 2 - rarely true
> 3 - occasionally true
> 4 - often true
> 5 - almost always true

_____ 1. I am extremely careful to avoid attacking individuals' intelligence when I attack their ideas.

_____ 2. When individuals are very stubborn, I use insults to soften the stubbornness.

_____ 3. I try very hard to avoid having other people feel bad about themselves when I try to influence them.

_____ 4. When people refuse to do a task I know is important, without good reason, I tell them they are unreasonable.

_____ 5. When others do things I regard as stupid, I try to be extremely gentle with them.

_____ 6. If individuals I am trying to influence really deserve it, I attack their character.

_____ 7. When people behave in ways that are in very poor taste, I insult them in order to shock them into proper behavior.

_____ 8. I try to make people feel good about themselves even when their ideas are stupid.

_____ 9. When people simply will not budge on a matter of importance I lose my temper and say rather strong things to them.

_____ 10. When people criticize my shortcomings, I take it in good humor and do not try to get back at them.

---

*From: Infante, D.A., & Wigley, C.J. (1986). Verbal aggressiveness: An interpersonal model and measure. *Communication Monographs, 53*, 61-69. Reproduced with permission of the authors.

_____ 11. When individuals insult me, I get a lot of pleasure out of really telling them off.

_____ 12. When I dislike individuals greatly, I try not to show it in what I say or how I say it.

_____ 13. I like poking fun at people who do things which are very stupid in order to stimulate their intelligence.

_____ 14. When I attack a persons' ideas, I try not to damage their self-concepts.

_____ 15. When I try to influence people, I make a great effort not to offend them.

_____ 16. When people do things which are mean or cruel, I attack their character in order to help correct their behavior.

_____ 17. I refuse to participate in arguments when they involve personal attacks.

_____ 18. When nothing seems to work in trying to influence others, I yell and scream in order to get some movement from them.

_____ 19. When I am not able to refute others' positions, I try to make them feel defensive in order to weaken their positions.

_____ 20. When an argument shifts to personal attacks, I try very hard to change the subject.

Appendix D

Verbal Aggressiveness Scoring

1. Add your scores on items: 2, 4, 6, 7, 9, 11, 13, 16, 18, 19
2. Add your scores on items: 1, 3, 5, 8, 10, 12, 14, 15, 17, 20
3. Subtract the sum obtained in step 2 from 60
4. To compute your verbal aggressiveness score, add the total obtained in step 1 to the result obtained in step 3

Interpretation:

59-100 = High in Verbal Aggressiveness

39-58 = Moderate in Verbal Aggressiveness

20-38 = Low in Verbal Aggressiveness

Appendix E

Debate Formats

Three debate formats are presented. The time limits are set so that a debate with four persons or two two-person debates will fit easily into a 50-minute class session. For a detailed account of the duties of each speaker see Wood (1968, pp. 180-82). Generally, the constructive speeches involve presenting one's case and attempting to refute the opponents' case. The rebuttal speeches are concerned with rebuilding one's case and continued attack on the opponents' case. Usually, the first affirmative constructive speaker deals with the major issues of Problem and Blame while the second affirmative constructive speaker argues the Solution and Consequences issues. The negative constructive speakers attempt to refute the affirmatives' arguments and they also present a defense of the status quo (unless they present a counterplan). No new issues should be introduced in the rebuttal speeches. The speakers should continue arguments which were begun in the constructive speeches. Notice that the affirmative always has the first and last word in a debate (this is a benefit of assuming the burden of proof).

Standard Debate

This is the most common form of educational debate. The four constructive speeches follow one another with no time in between speeches. There may be a short intermission after the constructive speeches to allow the partners to confer. The rebuttal speeches are then presented with no break between speeches.

Constructive Speeches

First Affirmative Speaker	7 minutes
First Negative Speaker	7 minutes
Second Affirmative Speaker	7 minutes
Second Negative Speaker	7 minutes

Rebuttal Speeches

First Negative Speaker	4 minutes
First Affirmative Speaker	4 minutes
Second Negative Speaker	4 minutes
Second Affirmative Speaker	4 minutes

Cross Examination Debate

This is a form of educational debate which simulates debate in a judicial setting since cross examination of speakers is involved. Once a constructive speech is finished the designated cross examining speaker arises and questions the constructive speaker.

Constructive Speeches

First Affirmative Speaker	5 minutes
Cross Examination by First Negative	3 minutes
First Negative Speaker	5 minutes
Cross Examination by Second Affirmative	3 minutes
Second Affirmative Speaker	5 minutes
Cross Examination by Second Negative	3 minutes
Second Negative Speaker	5 minutes
Cross Examination by First Affirmative	3 minutes

Rebuttal Speeches

First Negative Speaker	3 minutes
First Affirmative Speaker	3 minutes
Second Negative Speaker	3 minutes
Second Affirmative Speaker	3 minutes

Two Person Debate

This is the format used in the famous debates between Abraham Lincoln and Stephen Douglas. An interesting way to use this format is to allow the audience to question the speakers once the third speech is completed.

Affirmative Speaker	7 minutes
Negative Speaker	10 minutes
Affirmative Speaker	3 minutes

References

Adler, R.B. (1977). *Confidence in communication: A guide to assertive and social skills.* New York: Holt, Rinehart and Winston.

Alberti, R.E., & Emmons, M.L. (1974). *Your perfect right: A guide to assertive behavior* (2nd Ed.). San Luis Obispo, CA: Impact.

Bandura, A. (1973). *Aggression: A social learning analysis.* Englewood Cliffs, NJ: Prentice-Hall, Inc.

Berger, C.R., & Calabrese, R.J. (1975). Some exploration in initial interaction and beyond: Toward a developmental theory of interpersonal communication. *Human Communication Research, 1,* 99-112.

Berkowitz, L. (1962). *Aggression: A social psychological analysis.* New York: McGraw-Hill, Inc.

Bostrom, R.N. (1983). *Persuasion.* Englewood Cliffs, NJ: Prentice-Hall, Inc.

Burgoon, J.K., & Saine, T. (1978). *The unspoken dialogue: An introduction to nonverbal communication.* Boston: Houghton Mifflin Co.

Buss, A.H. (1961). *The psychology of aggression.* New York: John Wiley & Sons, Inc.

Cronkhite, G. (1969). *Persuasion: Speech and behavioral change.* Indianapolis: The Bobbs-Merrill Co., Inc.

Cronkhite, G., & Liska, J. (1976). A critique of factor analytic approaches to the study of credibility. *Communication Monographs, 43,* 91-107.

Delia, J.G. (1976). A constructivistic analysis of the concept of credibility. *Quarterly Journal of Speech, 62,* 361-375.

DeVito, J.A. (1986). *The interpersonal communication book* (4th Ed.). New York: Harper & Row, Publishers, Inc.

158   References

Eakins, B.W., & Eakins, R.G. (1978). *Sex differences in human communication*. Boston: Houghton Mifflin Co.
Folger, J.P., & Poole, M.S. (1984). *Working through conflict: A communication perspective*. Glenview, IL: Scott, Foresman & Co.
Freeley, A.J. (1966). *Argumentation and debate: Rational decision making* (2nd ed.). Belmont, CA: Wadsworth, Inc.
Gelles, R.J. (1974). *The violent home*. Beverly Hills, CA: Sage Publications, Inc.
Gorden, W.I., & Infante, D.A. (1987). Employee rights: Content, argumentativeness, verbal aggressiveness and career satisfaction. In C.A.B. Osigweh (Ed.), *Communicating employee responsibilities and rights: A modern management mandate*, (pp. 149-163). Westport, CT: Quorum Books, Greenwood Press.
Gorden, W.I., Infante, D.A., Wilson, L., & Clarke, C. (1984). Rationale and development of an employee rights scale. In H.L. Ewbank (Ed.), *Free Speech Yearbook 1984* (pp. 66-79). Annandale, VA: Speech Communication Association.
Gottman, J.M. (1979). *Marital interaction: Experimental investigations*. New York: Academic Press, Inc.
Greenberg, B.S., & Miller, G.R. (1966). The effects of low-credible sources on message acceptance. *Speech Monographs, 33*, 127-136.
Gulley, H. & Berlo, D. (1956). Effects of intercellular and intracellular speech structure on attitude change and learning. *Speech Monographs, 23*, 288-297.
Infante, D.A. (1971a). The influrnce of a topical system on the discovery or arguments. *Speech Monographs, 38*, 125-128.
Infante, D.A. (1971b). Predicting attitude from desirability and likelihood ratings of rhetorical propositions. *Speech Monographs, 38*, 321-326.
Infante, D.A. (1972a). Cognitive structure as a predictor of post speech attitude and attitude change. *Speech Monographs, 39*, 55-61.
Infante, D.A. (1972b). The function of perceptions of consequences in attitude formation and communicator image formation. *Central States Speech Journal, 23*, 174-180.
Infante, D.A. (1973). The perceived importance of cognitive structure components: An adaptation of Fishbein's theory. *Speech Monographs, 40*, 8-16.
Infante, D.A. (1975a). Differential functions of desirable and undesirable consequences in predicting attitude and attitude change toward proposals. *Speech Monographs, 42*, 115-134.
Infante, D.A. (1975b). The Socratic effect in responses to speeches opposing a proposal. *Central States Speech Journal, 26*, 201-206.

Infante, D.A. (1977). Cognitive behaviors and interpersonal communication. In T.M. Steinfatt (Ed.), Readings in human communication: An interpersonal introduction (pp. 243-265). Indianapolis: Bobbs-Merrill Co., Inc.

Infante, D.A. (1978). Similarity between advocate and receiver: The role of instrumentality. Central States Speech Journal, 29, 187-193.

Infante, D.A. (1980). The construct validity of semantic differential scales for the measurement of source credibility. Communication Quarterly, 28, 19-26.

Infante, D.A. (1981). Trait argumentativeness as a predictor of communicative behavior in situations requiring argument. Central States Speech Journal, 32, 265-272.

Infante, D.A. (1982). The argumentative student in the speech communication classroom: An investigation and implications. Communication Education, 31, 141-148.

Infante, D.A. (1983). Motivation to speak on a controversial topic: Value-expectancy, sex differences, and implications. Central States Speech Journal, 34, 96-103.

Infante, D.A. (1985). Influencing women to be more argumentative: Source credibility effects. Journal of Applied Communication Research, 13, 33-44.

Infante, D.A. (1987). Aggressivensss. In J.C. McCroskey and J.A. Daly (Eds.). Personality and interpersonal communication, (pp. 157-192). Newbury Park, CA: Sage Publications, Inc.

Infante, D.A. (in press). Enhancing the prediction of response to a communication situation from communication traits. Communication Quarterly.

Infante, D.A., & Fisher, J.Y. (1978). Anticipated credibility and message strategy intentions as predictors of trait and state speech anxiety. Central States Speech Journal, 29, 1-10.

Infante, D.A., & Gorden, W.I. (1981). Similarities and differences in the communicator styles of superiors and subordinates: Relations to subordinate satisfaction. Communication Quarterly, 30, 67-71.

Infante, D.A., & Gorden, W.I. (1985a). Superiors' argumentativeness and verbal aggressiveness as predictors of subordinates' satisfaction. Human Communication Research, 12, 117-125.

Infante, D.A., & Gorden, W.I. (1985b). Benefits versus bias: An investigation of argumentativeness, gender, and organizational communication outcomes. Communication Research Reports, 2, 196-201.

Infante, D.A., & Grimmett, R.A. (1971). Attitudinal effects of utilizing a critical method of analysis. Central States Speech Journal, 22, 213-217.

Infante, D.A., Heinan-Wall, C., Leap, C.J., & Danielson, K. (1984).
Verbal aggression as a function of the receiver's argumentativeness. Communication Research Reports, 1, 33-37.

Infante, D.A., Parker, K.R., Clarke, C.H., Wilson, L., & Nathu, I.A.
(1983). A comparison of factor and functional approaches to
source credibility. Communication Quarterly, 31, 43-48.

Infante, D.A., & Rancer, A.S. (1982). A conceptualization and measure
of argumentativeness. Journal of Personality Assessment, 46, 72-
80.

Infante, D.A., Trebing, J.D., Shepherd, P.E., & Seeds, D.E. (1984). The
Relationship of argumentativeness to verbal aggression. Southern
Speech Communication Journal, 50, 67-77.

Infante, D.A., & Wigley, C.J. (1986). Verbal aggressiveness: An interpersonal model and measure. Communication Monographs, 53, 61-
69.

Jandt, F.E. (1973). Conflict resolution through communication. New
York: Harper & Row, Publishers, Inc.

Jensen, J.V. (1981). Argumentation: Reasoning in Communication. New
York: D. Van Nostrand.

Johnson, D.W., & Johnson, R.T. (1979). Conflict in the classroom: Controversy and learning. Review of Educational Research, 49, 51-70.

Johnson, D.W., & Johnson, R.T. (1985). Classroom conflict: Controversy
versus debate in learning groups. American Education Research
Journal, 22, 237-256.

Jourard, S.M. (1968). Disclosing man to himself. New York: Van
Nostrand Reinhold Co., Inc.

Jourard, S.M. (1971). The transparent self (rev. ed.). New York: Van
Nostrand Reinhold Co., Inc.

Knapp, M.L. (1980). Essentials of nonverbal communication. New York:
Holt, Rinehart and Winston.

Maccoby, E.M., & Jacklin, C.N. (1974). The psychology of sex differences. Stanford: Stanford University Press.

McCroskey, J.C. (1969). A summary of experimental research on the
effects of evidence in persuasive communication. Quarterly
Journal of Speech, 55, 169-176.

McCroskey, J.C., Richmond, V.P., & Daly, J.A. (1975). The development
of a measure of perceived homophily in interpersonal communication. Human Communication Research, 1, 323-332.

Miller, G.A. (1956). The magic number seven, plus or minus two: Some
limits to our capacity for processing information. Psychological
Review, 62, 81-97.

Miller, G., Boster, F., Roloff, M., & Seibold, D. (1977). Compliance-
gaining message strategies: A typology and some findings con-

References

161

cerning effects of situational differences. *Communication Monographs, 44,* 37-51.

Mills, G.E. (1968). *Reason in controversy* (2nd ed.). Boston, MA: Allyn and Bacon, Inc.

Moine, D.J. (1982). To trust, perchance to buy. *Psychology Today, 16,* 50-54.

Nelson, W.F. (1970). Topoi: Functional in human recall. *Speech Monographs, 37,* 121-126.

Nemeth, C.J. (1986). Differential contributions of majority and minority influence. *Psychological Review, 93,* 23-32.

Onyekwere, E.O. (1986). The effects of argumentativeness, ego-involvement, and gender on perceived interpersonal competence. Doctoral dissertation, Kent State University.

Ostermeier, T. (1967). Effects of type and frequency of reference upon perceived source credibility and attitude change. *Speech Monographs, 34,* 137-144.

Pearson, J.C. (1985). *Gender and communication.* Dubuque, IA: Wm. C. Brown Group.

Rancer, A.S., Baukus, R.A., & Amato, P.P. (1986). Argumentativeness, verbal aggressiveness and marital satisfaction. *Communication Research Reports, 3,* 28-32.

Rancer, A.S., Baukus, R.A., & Infante, D.A. (1985). Relations between argumentativeness and belief structures about arguing. *Communication Education, 34,* 37-47.

Rancer, A.S., & Dierks-Stewart, K.J. (1985). The influence of sex and sex-role orientation on trait argumentativeness. *Journal of Personality Assessment, 49,* 69-70.

Rancer, A.S., & Infante, D.A. (1985). Relations between motivation to argue and the argumentativeness of adversaries. *Communication Quarterly, 33,* 209-218.

Schultz, B. (1982). Argumentativeness: Its effect in group decision-making and its role in leadership perception. *Communication Quarterly, 30,* 368-375.

Thistlethwaite, D.L., & Kamenetsky, J. (1955). Attitude change through refutation and elaboration of audience counter-arguments. *Journal of Abnormal and Social Psychology, 51,* 3-12.

Toch, H. (1969). *Violent men.* Chicago: Aldine Publishing Co.

Toulmin, S. (1958). *The uses of argument.* Cambridge: Cambridge University Press.

Tubbs, S. (1968). Explicit versus implicit audience conclusions and audience commitment. *Speech Monographs, 35,* 14-19.

Vuchinich, S. (1985). Arguments, family style. *Psychology Today, 19,* 40-46.

Wheeless, L. (1973). Effects of explicit credibility statements by a more credible or a less credible source. *Southern Speech Communication Journal, 39,* 33-39.

Wheeless, L.R., & Grotz, J. (1976). Conceptualization and measurement of reported self-disclosure. *Human Communication Research, 2,* 338-346.

Wheeless, L.R., & Grotz, J. (1977). The measurement of trust and its relationship to self-disclosure. *Human Communication Research, 3,* 250-257.

Wilmot, J.H., & Wilmot, W.W. (1978). *Interpersonal conflict.* Dubuque, IA: Wm. C. Brown Group.

Windes, R.R., & Hastings. A. (1965). *Argumentation and advocacy.* New York: Random House, Inc.

Wood, R.V. (1968). *Strategic debate.* Skokie, IL: National Textbook Co.

Ziegelmuller, G.W., & Dause, C.A. (1975). *Argumentation: Inquiry and advocacy.* Englewood Cliffs, NJ: Prentice-Hall, Inc.

Zillman, D. (1979). *Hostility and aggression.* Hillsdale, NJ: Lawrence Erlbaum Associates, Inc.

Index

163

Index

165